ST. PETERSBURG

SAINT PETERSBURG

SAINT PETERSBURG

Text

Natalia Popova

Translation

Gillian Kenyon

Design

Nikolai Kutovoy

Photographs

Vladimir Antoshchenkov,
Valentin Baranovsky, Nikolai Berketov,
Leonid Bogdanov, Serguei Chistobaev,
Vladimir Davydov, Pavel Demidov,
Vladimir Denisov, Vladimir Dorokhov,
Vadim Egorovsky, Vladimir Filippov,
Leonid Gerkus, Eduard Gorbatenko,
Valery Gordt, Pavel Ivanov,
Leonard Kheifets, Artur Kirakozov,
Boris Manushin, Vladimir Melnikov,
Yury Molodkovets, Alexander Petrosian,
Serguei Podmiotin, Nikolai Rakhmanov,
Alexander Riazantsev, Viktor Savik,
Georgy Shablovsky, Vladimir Shirokov,
Vladimir Shlakan, Evgueny Shlepkin,
Evgueny Siniaver, Vladimir Terebenin,
Oleg Trubsky, Vasily Vorontsov,
Kira Zharinova

Editors

Irina Kharitonova, Irina Lvova

English text editor

Elena Shabalova

Computer layout

Tatiana Krakovskaya

Colour correction

Viacheslav Bykovski, Vladimir Kniazev,
Alexander Kondratov, Tatiana Krakovskaya
Alexander Miagkov, Dmitry Trofimov

ISBN 5-93893-284-X

Printed and bound in Russia

M. Makhaev
View of the River Neva.
1753. Engraving

The city of St Petersburg, the former capital of the Russian Empire and the embodiment of the pride and glory of the Russian state, was founded on 27 May 1703. The creation of the city was a daring feat. In order to realise his vision, Peter I, turning his back on the traditions of "ancient" Rus, called upon the new generation, which, with its fierce confidence and characteristic youthfulness, welcomed his ambitious plans. St Petersburg became the symbol of a new era of Russian history and grandiose, unprecedented ventures. As if challenging nature itself, the Emperor resolved to create a northern "Paradise" on an area of marshy land that seemed perpetually wreathed in mist. Petersburg became the primary concern and favourite "child of the northern giant, in which the energy, brutality and revolutionary force of the '93 Convention were concentrated, … [the favourite child] of the tsar, who renounced his country for its own good and oppressed it in the name of Europeanism and civilisation" (Alexander Herzen). Indeed, the building of the new capital demanded a concerted effort and a great deal of strength. Many thousands of human lives were lost in the process, and it is perhaps because of this that the history

of Petersburg is so full of dark and tragic events. During the three hundred years of its existence, it has endured more than its fair share of historical and natural disasters.

In times of war, hostile forces have tried again and again to capture the city, thinking to erase it from the face of the earth, but not once has an army succeeded in setting foot within its limits. Even the most terrifying blockade in the history of mankind, lasting 872 days from 8 September 1941 to 27 January 1944, was unable to break the spirit of the city's inhabitants.

In the autumn, the merciless elements threaten to wreak havoc on the long, flat banks of the River Neva. Three terrible deluges, which have occurred with an alarming regularity every hundred years (1724, 1824 and 1924), and other less significant floods have sought to destroy this manmade wonder, yet the city has stood its ground.

St Petersburg is the "strangest of all Russian cities." It is a unique entity with a highly pronounced individuality and a complex and subtle spirit, which leads a mysterious, dramatic life of its own. No other Russian city is the subject of so many myths and legends. No other city has aroused such mixed responses from the very moment it was born: it has been loved and hated, lauded and damned, but it has left no one indifferent. "What a city! What a river! An unparalleled city! One must part with Petersburg for a short time and see the old capitals, ramshackle Paris and sooty London, in order to appreciate Petersburg's worth. Look what harmony! How all the parts complement the whole! Such beautiful buildings, such taste and altogether such variety springing from the union of water and buildings." Dating from the early 19th century, these are the words of the famous Russian poet Konstantin Batiushkov, a man with a keen sense of the beauty of Petersburg. The reason why this most "contrived" city is so remarkable is that "its appearance bears the mark of a deliberate human creation." It began with thoughts and ideas laid out in a plan. The open stretches of dry land and the lines of the Neva and the canals became formative elements in the design of Petersburg. Here, emphasis was placed less on erecting individual buildings than on creating entire artificial panoramas. Architects were careful to contrive long vistas. The idiosyncrasies of the design of the northern capital can be seen clearly from a bird's eye view. "Everything appears flat, the city's unevenness is erased, and before us lies a faintly outlined relief, like a plan. Yet the observer is able to see the city within the framework of nature. It is as if nature is closing in on the city, while the city casts its reflection on the surrounding landscape" (Nikolai Antsiferov).

Benjamin Patersen. *Peter's Square.* 1806. Engraving

Vasily Sadovnikov *Square between St Isaac's and the Admiralty.* 1847. Watercolour

Axonometric view of St Isaac's

St Isaac's Cathedral, one of the most prominent features of the St Petersburg skyline, towers over St Isaac's Square and Decembrists' (formerly Senate) Square on the left bank of the Neva. Its gilded dome is visible even from the city's remote outskirts. In earlier days the heavy peals of the large bell of Russia's main cathedral and the ringing of its four belfries' numerous bells resounded as far as the Gulf of Finland. St Isaac's is the fourth largest domed cathedral in the world after St Peter's in Rome, St Paul's in London and Sta Maria del Fiore in Florence.

St Isaac's, amazing for its sheer size even by modern standards, is 101.5 m high, 111.3 m long (with porticoes) and 97.6 m wide. The inner diameter of the dome is 21.8 m and the outer diameter 25.8 m. The pediments rest on 112 monolithic granite columns — each portico column is 17 m high and weighs 114 tons. The cathedral can accommodate about 14,000 people. St Isaac's Cathedral was designed by Auguste Ricard de Montferrand, an outstanding French architect in the first half of the nineteenth century, who came to Russia at the age of thirty. His career took off almost immediately on his arrival in St Petersburg largely due to the patronage of Augustin de Béthencourt, the leading engineer of that period who headed the Committee for Construction and Hydraulic Works in St Petersburg.

Petersburg also owes its uniqueness to its geographical location: it stands on the edge of the vast territory of Russia and is indeed a "window onto Europe". From the west it has not only been buffeted by the waters of the autumn floods, but also by the shocks of historic disasters endured by the West. European ideas and the joys and woes of the "old continent" have been borne in on the Baltic winds.

St Petersburg threw its doors open wide to everyone who accepted the invitation to take part in the ambitious and rather risky business of its creation. The young city was notable for its receptivity to the cultural achievements of Europe and the knowledge and skills of its foreign guests. In other countries, schools were established first, followed by universities, and only once a significant number of scholars had emerged were academies founded. In Peter's day, the first schools were only beginning to take shape in Russia and not a single university existed, yet the tsar-reformer had already decided to invite learned foreigners (mainly from Germany) to Petersburg to create an Academy of Sciences. He offered them the opportunity

to conduct scientific research at the expense of the state in return for introducing young Russian men to the principles of science. Artists, architects, sculptors and engravers were also invited to Russia to sow the seeds of the European fine arts in the damp soil on the banks of the Neva. Petersburg swiftly absorbed and assimilated all things beautiful. Germans, Swedes, Italians, Dutch-, French- and Englishmen initially made their homes in separate colonies, but the national and linguistic boundaries gradually disappeared. Within a short time, a unique nation had arisen – the nation of Petersburg, in which locals and Russified foreigners lived in harmony. For many who came to Petersburg, the city became a second home to which they devoted their energy and talents. Together with Russian experts, they worked to create a city and build splendid country residences for the ruling elite. Some people believe that "Petersburg doesn't have an ounce of originality: it is simply a kind of general embodiment of the notion of a capital city, and is the spit and image of any other major city in the world" (Vissarion Belinsky).

Basiolli.
Neva as viewed from Peter and Paul Fortress. 1830s. Lithography

Karl Beggrov.
General Staff building. 1822. Lithography

Church of the Resurrection on the Blood

Cross section of the church

It has long been a tradition in Russian architecture to erect religious buildings in honour of historic events. The Church in the Name of the Resurrection of Christ on the Site of the Mortal Wounding of His Honoured Majesty Alexander II, as the church's canonical title reads, stands on the exact spot where the emperor was fatally injured on 1 March 1881 by a bomb thrown by the radical, Ignaty Grinevitsky. It is more commonly known as the Church of the Saviour on the Spilled Blood. It would be more accurate, however, to call it the Church

Yet nothing could be further from the truth. European architectural forms metamorphosed under the influences of Russian architecture, resulting in the emergence of genuinely unique edifices. In art, as in the social and everyday life of the city, European and Russian traditions merged to create an entirely new phenomenon – the culture of St Petersburg.

Saint Petersburg saw in the 21st century in all its majestic beauty, emphasising its significance as a unique museum of urban planning and architecture. For the residents of Petersburg, however, the city has been and continues first and foremost to be their home. Descendants of the craftsmen who began to build Petersburg under Peter I live and work here. Through their efforts, the city continues to grow and, thus, new quarters emerge.

In contradistinction to other European capitals, Saint Petersburg has only been on the map for three hundred years. Its beauty, however, has long since earned it worldwide acclaim, and it rivals such international centres as London and Paris in terms of its fame. Tourists can often detect elements of other European cities in Saint Petersburg: its embankments are reminiscent of Paris and its many canals reminiscent of Amsterdam. The countless bridges and the tangible sense of proximity to the sea bring to mind Venice, while shades of London are to be found in the city's mists and green parks. Yet for all these similarities, Petersburg, like its counterparts, is unique and extraordinary. Even after just a single visit, it is impossible to forget the splendour of its architectural ensembles, the idiosyncratic beauty of the streets and houses of "informal" Petersburg, the ghostly charm of the White Nights, the sparkling jets of the Peterhof fountains on a bright summer's day, the gold and scarlet of the autumnal parks, or the dazzling brilliance of the winter snows.

of the Resurrection on the Blood, since it was consecrated in the name of the Resurrection of Christ rather than in the name of Christ the Saviour. This striking edifice is one of the few remaining examples of late 19th – early 20th century religious architecture in Russia and today represents a commemorative monument of both historic and artistic value.

Palace Square seen from the roof of the Winter Palace

THE PETER AND PAUL FORTRESS

For the first few years, construction work was centred on Hare Island. Here, the fortress of Sankt Pieter Burkh was erected as the nucleus of the future city. Its location was selected by Peter the Great himself who well understood the strategic advantages of placing such an outpost on the island in the Neva delta. Within a year, six bastions (the projecting portions of a fortification) had been raised. Although the bastions were made of earth (substituted with stone in 1740), building the new city out of stone was one of Peter's greatest concerns. A special decree was issued prohibiting the construction of stone edifices elsewhere in Russia, and all master stonemasons were ordered to the banks of the Neva. Peter also introduced an unusual "stone toll": every boat and every string of carts to enter the city had to bring a certain number of stones with it.

The fortress was designed as a closed rampart consisting of bastions and curtains (the part of the wall connecting the bastions). Peter was in a hurry to complete the job before the winter and so the construction of the fortifications was carried out under the supervision of the tsar's closest associates, thus the bastions are named in honour of these men, to wit, Naryshkin,

1. Peter and Paul Fortress. Bird's-eye view

2. St Peter's Gate. The "state eagle" of Russia. Detail of the decoration

Trubetskoy, Zotov, Golovkin and Menshikov. One of the southern bastions was built under the direct observation of Peter himself and consequently became known as the Tsar Bastion. On the eastern side of the island, in the curtain that links the Tsar Bastion with the Menshikov Bastion, the main gates to the fortress – St Peter's Gate – were installed. They were protected by a ravelin (a V-shaped outwork incorporated into the design of the ramparts), which was named in honour of Saint John. In order to get into the fortress it was necessary to cross the wooden St John's Bridge, pass through St John's Gate and then through a second gateway – St Peter's Gate (built in stone to replace the original wooden structure in 1714–1718, architect: Domenico Trezzini). The triumphal arch of the latter still bears a beautifully preserved double-headed eagle (the coat-of-arms of the Russian Empire) wearing imperial crowns, made of lead and weighing over a tonne. Beyond St Peter's Gate the path is lined

3

3. St Peter's Gate.
1714–1718, architect:
Domenico Trezzini
sculptors: Hans Konrad
Osner, Nicolas Pinod

4. View of St John's Bridge
and St John's Gate

by two squat military buildings: to the right is the Artillery Arsenal (1801), and to the left is the Engineer's House (1749).

By 1787, the entire fortress was clad in granite. A signal tower and flagpole for a special fortress standard, were installed on the Naryshkin Bastion, which also became the site of a cannon, fired every day at noon, a tradition that has been preserved to this day.

Not far from the Sts Peter and Paul Cathedral is the Commandant's House (1743–1746) in which the commanding officer of the fortress lived. Over the course of two hundred years there were 32 commandants. It was an honoured position and was often held for life. It was awarded to generals of great merit who had earned the particular trust of the sovereign. In one of the rooms of the Commandant's House, now the Memorial Hall, the Supreme Criminal Court would convene to hear the cases of the many political prisoners held in the Peter and Paul Fortress.

5

5. Trubetskoi Bastion

9

6, 7, 9. Peter and Paul Fortress.
1712–1733, architect: Domenico Trezzini

8. The bells of the Flemish carillon

7

THE STS PETER AND PAUL CATHEDRAL

The main building within the fortress is the Sts Peter and Paul Cathedral. Its shape is somewhat reminiscent of that of an 18th century ship: the high eastern wall is the stern, while the tall spire is the mast. This belfry together with the gilded spire and figure of an angel, the guardian of the city, stands at a height of 122.5 metres. At the time it was the tallest building in Russia. The figure of the angel serves as a weather vane, indicating the direction of the wind. Stretching boldly towards the heavens, the cathedral spire became an integral part of the Petersburg skyline from the moment it first appeared. The design of the church, including the decorative fittings inside, is indicative of the typical Petersburg practice of combining the traditions of western religious architecture and Ancient Russian church design. Thus, the interior of the cathedral includes both a carved wooden iconostasis executed after the Orthodox traditions, and a carved pulpit for the preacher, as in a Catholic church.

8

10

11

12

10, 11. Sts Peter and Paul Cathedral.
Iconostasis. Icons: *Queen Bathsheba,
Holy Prince St Alexander Nevsky*.
Mid-18th century, artists: Alexei
Protopopov, Andrei Pospelov

12. Tsar's place and the pulpit

13. Interior

14. Iconostasis. 1722–1729,
designed by Ivan Zarudny
and Domenico Trezzini

15. Life-giving altar cross.
Re-created in 1994–95 after
drawings by Andrei Nartov.
Ivory, wood, gilded bronze

16. Tsar's Gate. Detail

14

15   16

17

18

19

The interior of the cathedral is designed like a ceremonial hall, divided by piers into three naves. Its main feature is the carved gilded iconostasis (1722–1729, designed by the architects Domenico Trezzini and Ivan Zarudny). The central section of the iconostasis resembles a triumphal arch, a symbolic celebration of the glorious victory of the Russian troops in the Northern War. The lavishness and grandeur of the architectural forms of this altar screen combined with countless sculptures creates the kind of stunning decorative effect that is typical of the Baroque style. Beyond the *tsarskie vrata* (*the tsar's gates* or central doors in the iconostasis) there is a richly decorated canopy over the table used in the performance of religious ceremonies. It was fashioned after Lorenzo Bernini's canopy in St Peter's Cathedral in Rome.

In the 1830s, in the right-hand row of piers, the *imperial (tsar's) place* was installed, made up of a small dais under a carved wooden canopy where the Emperor or Empress would stand during services. The canopy is decorated with drapes of raspberry velvet and its carved peak is crowned with the representation of a pillow bearing the royal regalia. Opposite the *tsar's place* is the pulpit, decorated with wooden statues of the Apostles Peter and Paul, the four Evangelists and the Holy Spirit in the form of a dove surrounded by clouds and cherubim. The pulpit is additionally decorated with paintings on Gospel subjects. This splendid example of Russian woodcarving was installed here in 1732.

The Sts Peter and Paul Cathedral contains a significant collection of paintings from the Petrine era. The face of the iconostasis incorporates 43 icons, set out somewhat differently to those in the Russian Orthodox churches. The royal gates themselves are unusual – four panels covered with depictions of the Last Supper in bas-relief, and not a single icon in sight.

The cathedral is the imperial burial-vault. The tomb of Peter the Great is marked with the standards of the regiments which, under his leadership, conquered the Swedes in the Northern War (1700–1721). All of the Emperors and Grand Dukes lie under identical white marble sarcophagi, save for Alexander II and his wife Maria Alexandrovna, who was born a princess of Hessen-Darmstadt. Their graves are marked by sarcophagi made of coloured jasper by the workers of the Urals' plants as a sign of their gratitude for the abolition of serfdom.

In 1998, the remains of the last Russian Emperor, Nicholas II, and the various members of his family who were shot to death in Ekaterinburg in June 1918, were buried in the cathedral.

The Peter and Paul Fortress never served a direct military purpose, since no enemy ever made it as far as its walls. Very soon after it had been built, however, it began

17. The tomb of Peter the Great

18. Jean-Marc Nattier.
Portrait of Peter the Great. 1717

19. Nikolai Lavrov. *Alexander II.* 1860

20. Tombs of Alexander II and his wife Empress Maria Alexandrovna

21. Emperor Nicholas II and his family. 1904

22. St Catherine Chapel of the SS Peter and Paul Cathedral. Tomb of Emperor Nicholas II, Empress Alexandra Fiodorovna, their children and members of the household

21

22

23. Nikolai Gay.
*Peter the Great
Interrogates
the Tsarevich Alexis
at Peterhof.* 1871

24. The Trubetskoi
Bastion Prison

25. Konstantin Flavitsky.
Princess Tarakanova.
1864

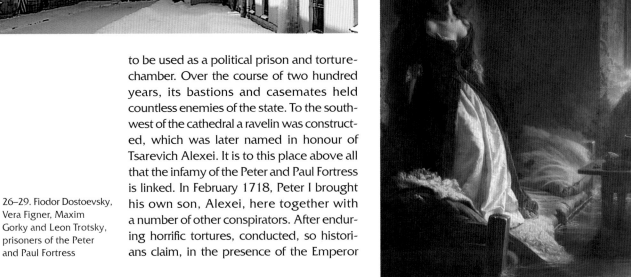

himself, Alexei was executed. Throughout the 18th century, many people experienced the horrors of the fortress's casemates. In 1775, on the orders of Catherine the Great a woman claiming to be the daughter of Empress Elizabeth Petrovna and a granddaughter of Peter the Great, was brought to the prison of the Peter and Paul Fortress. Although the prisoner died of tuberculosis, there emerged a legend that she perished during a flood and it was this legend that inspired a famous painting. In the 19th century, the chambers in the bastions and the Secret House of the Alexeevsky Ravelin built in the reign of Paul I were never empty.

26–29. Fiodor Dostoevsky, Vera Figner, Maxim Gorky and Leon Trotsky, prisoners of the Peter and Paul Fortress

to be used as a political prison and torture-chamber. Over the course of two hundred years, its bastions and casemates held countless enemies of the state. To the south-west of the cathedral a ravelin was constructed, which was later named in honour of Tsarevich Alexei. It is to this place above all that the infamy of the Peter and Paul Fortress is linked. In February 1718, Peter I brought his own son, Alexei, here together with a number of other conspirators. After enduring horrific tortures, conducted, so historians claim, in the presence of the Emperor

26

27

28

29

30

31

30, 31. Historical
exhibition of the
"Trubetskoi Bastion
Prison". The cell and
the corridor

32. 19th-century
shackles, prison
clothing and shoes
in the display the
"Trubetskoi Bastion
Prison"

32

In April 1849, for example, a large number of men who had been arrested in connection with the case of Buta-shevich-Petrashevsky were brought here, including the twenty-eight year old Dostoevsky. One of the many places of incarceration that existed at different times within the fortress was the prison in the Trubetskoy Bastion (1708–1714). Those who died in solitary confinement within its walls, plagued by the stench and the damp, heard the melodious chimes of the Sts Peter and Paul Cathedral before they died. The last prisoners to be held in the Trubetskoy Bastion, from 1917–1919, were the ministers of the Provisional Government and the Grand Dukes.

In 1992, a statue of Peter I was erected on the square in front of the guardhouse and soon became the subject of great debate. This unusual image is quite different to the typical representations of the tsar-creator and tsar-victor that prevailed in the monumental sculptures of centuries gone by. Yet the longer the statue "lives" in the fortress, the more normal its presence becomes. Peter calmly observes the inquisitive tourists, poses for their cameras and pays no attention to the children who today know no fear of the "bronze shadow" of the formidable Emperor.

33. Statue of Peter I. 1992, sculptor: Mikhail Shemiakin

34. Naryshkin Bastion

35. Spit of Vasilievsky Island and the Peter and Paul Fortress

33

VASILIEVSKY ISLAND

Petersburg is at once united and divided by the Neva. In May, the ice floes from Lake Ladoga in the east drift past the columned façades of the city's palaces, bringing a cold northeastern wind with them. Since the time of Peter the Great, the Neva has been linked to the basin of the mighty Volga by a system of waterways. It is as if the cares of the vast territory of Russia, reaching right back to the Pacific, are carried along with the drifting ice and the winds from the east. As it wends its smooth and leisurely way, the Neva assumes a number of very different guises. From the Lieutenant Schimdt and Tuchkov Bridges right up to the Smolny Convent it is a stately,

cosmopolitan river. Here, all of the architectural beauty of old Petersburg is to be seen lining its banks. Up to these bridges and beyond the Smolny stretches the working river, marked by the cranes of the freight port, the masts of boats in the shipyards and the industrial chimneys at the mouth of the Neva. By day, the Neva is quiet and majestic. Freight transportation within the city limits has almost ceased, smoky long boats no longer moor along the embankments, and the lumbering barges that once travelled the lengths of the Neva, the Nevka, the Fontanka and the Moika have given way to modern ocean liners, antique sailboats and floating restaurants in the guise of old vessels. Likewise, the so-called "water trams" that once served the city's

36. Panoramic view of the Neva and Vasilievsky Island

37

37. Peter and Paul Fortress
from the Spit of Vasilievsky Island

38. Spit of Vasilievsky Island
seen from the Palace Embankment

38

internal waterways have been replaced by motorboats of various sizes carrying cargoes of sightseers. After it had been decreed in 1712 that the imperial court was to move from Moscow to the banks of the Neva, the northern city began to be developed in accordance with a plan that had been drawn up previously by local and foreign experts. Vasilievsky Island was originally intended to become the heart of the emerging city. Peter was particularly fond of Amsterdam and hoped that the new capital would somehow remind him of that place.

40

39, 40. Rostral Column. 1805–1810, sculptors: Georges Camberlain, François Thibault. 1810, architect: Jean-François Thomas de Thomon

41

42

43

STOCK EXCHANGE
KUNSTKAMMER

For a hundred years Vasilievsky Island was the site of the city's port. At the beginning of the 19th century, it was moved further downstream, and now only the wrought iron rings set in the granite walls of the embankment serve as a reminder of the fact that ships once moored here. The spit of Vasilievsky Island was designed to reflect Petersburg's status as an international centre of shipping and commerce. The centrepiece of the resulting architectural composition is the Stock Exchange, which resembles a Doric-style temple, hence its nickname the "Russian Parthenon". The main façade, overlooking the Neva, is adorned with the figures of the sea god Neptune and his retinue, while on the western side an allegorical embodiment of Navigation stands alongside the god of commerce, Mercury. Although Mercury is no longer worshipped here, the building remains faithful to the fierce god of the sea: today, the Stock Exchange is the home of the Naval Museum.

The first building to be constructed facing the Neva during the Petrine era was the *Kunstkammer*, which became the city's first public museum.

45

46

44

41, 42. Exhibits from the Peter the Great Anthropological and Ethnological Museum

43. Institute of Russian Literature ("Pushkin House"). 1829–1832, architect: Giovanni Luchini

44. View of the University Embankment. *Kunstkammer* (now, Peter the Great Anthropological and Ethnological Museum). 1718–1734, architects: Georg Mattarnovi, Gaetano Chiaveri and Mikhail Zemtsov

45. Stock Exchange (Naval Museum). 1805–1816, architect: Jean-François Thomas de Thomon

46. Naval Museum display inside the Stock Exchange

47. Unknown
18th-century artist.
*Portrait of Alexander
Menshikov*

48. Grand Hall

49. Menshikov Palace.
1710s–1720s, architects:
Giovanni Mario Fontana,
Gottfried Johann Schaedel

50. University
Embankment. Pier in front
of the Academy of Arts.
1832–1834, architect:
Konstantin Thon.
Sphinx (Egypt,
13th century B.C.)

47

48

49

THE MENSHIKOV PALACE

In the early 18th century, the city's first and largest estate, the property of Peter I's close associate and the first governor of Petersburg, Alexander Menshikov, was built. Today, only the palace remains, overlooking the Neva and equipped with its own pier. The only one of its kind in Petersburg at the time, the palace was used to receive ambassadors and host the Petersburg "assemblies" at which Peter the Great taught European etiquette to the boyars who had moved north from Moscow. The palace grew together with the city. The palace has survived to this day with very few changes and is now a valuable monument to the architecture of the first third of the 18th century.

51. Academy of Arts Museum. Copies of ancient sculptures

52. Rumiantsev Obelisk in the Rumiantsev Gardens. 1799, architect: Vincenzo Brenna, sculptor: Pierre-Louis Agie

53. Academy of Arts. 1764–1788, architects: Jean-Baptiste Vallin de La Mothe, Alexander Kokorinov

51

50

THE ACADEMY OF FINE ARTS

The building was erected after the founding of the Academy (1757) on the site of the houses of Petrine dignitaries. For a number of years, classes were actually held in these homes. The Petersburg Academy of Fine Arts was the first educational establishment of its type in Russia. To this day, Russian artists, sculptors and architects are trained there. In the early 19th century, a flight of granite steps leading down to the water was created in front of the Academy after designs by the architect Konstantin Thon. Since 1834, the stretch of embankment before the majestic bulk of the Academy of Arts has been guarded by a pair of sphinxes with the face of Amenhotep III, who was in power when the kingdom of Egypt was flourishing.

52

53

VASILIEVSKY ISLAND – THE MARITIME HEART OF ST PETERSBURG

It was planned to create a network of streets and canals, which would drain the marshy land, on Vasilievsky Island. Although this project was not brought to completion, the right-angled arrangement of the streets and the three main avenues which form the

54

55

56

architectural basis of the area today almost coincides with the initial plan. The so-called Bolshoy (Large), Sredny (Medium), and Maly (Small) Prospekts run from west to east and are intersected from north to south by 34 "lines", which open out onto the Neva. The abundance of water and the open skies above the flat, cheerless banks of the river, broken by the mouths of countless smaller channels, set the tone for the architectural development of Petersburg and determined its regular layout. Pride of place was given to the main waterway, the Neva. Downstream from the Lieutenant Schmidt Bridge, freight ships, tankers and tourist liners from far and wide line the banks of Vasilievsky Island and the English Embankment. On very rare occasions, when Petersburg happens to be one of the finishing points of the international Cutty Sark Tall Ships' Races, the river becomes crowded with sailboats and the façades of the elegant residences lining the banks are obscured by a forest of masts and rigging.

54. View of the Lieutenant Schmidt Bridge and the English Embankment

55. Lieutenant Schmidt Embankment. Statue of Admiral Krusenstern. 1873, sculptor: Ivan Schroeder

56. View of the English Embankment

57. International Cutty Sark Tall Ships' Races on the Neva

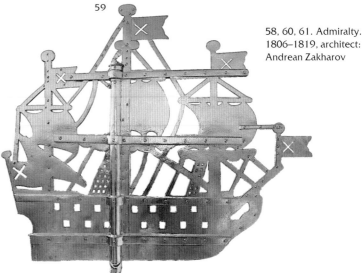

58, 60, 61. Admiralty.
1806–1819, architect:
Andrean Zakharov

nal plans for the Admiralty and replaced the frame-built warehouses with stone buildings. Moreover, he masterminded the construction of a tower with a tall gilded spire (now, 72 m high) topped with a weather vane in the shape of a three-sailed frigate. At the beginning of the 19th century, the Admiralty underwent fundamental reconstruction under the watchful eye of Andrean Zakharov. The Classical architect, while preserving Korobov's original concept, considerably

59. Caravel at the top of the Admiralty spire, one of the symbols of St Petersburg

62. Admiralty Embankment. Statue of Peter the Carpenter. 1880, sculptor: Leopold Bernstam

58

THE ADMIRALTY

In 1704, on Admiralty Island, situated on the left bank of the Neva and bordered to the south by the Moika, work began on the building of a shipyard that was designed by Peter the Great himself. Together with the Peter and Paul Fortress, the Admiralty Shipyard became one of the city's main architectural features. In the 1730s, the architect Ivan Korobov abandoned the origi-

60

enlarged the building and enhanced its appearance using sculptural designs. The New Admiralty was envisaged as a unique monument to the Russian fleet, thus its main entrance was given the form of a triumphal arch. Zakharov repeated the motif of the wide archway in the façades of the two symmetrically placed pavilions that face the Neva. The sculptural embellishments that indicate the purpose served by the Admiralty play an important part in the composition of the building as a whole. The idea of the synthesis of architecture and sculpture was central to Classical design and was first clearly demonstrated in Zakharov's work. He presented sculpture in all its manifestations, from freestanding statues to sculpted ornament, united by a single theme – the glorification of Russia's naval prowess. On the attic of the Admiralty tower, *The Establishment of a Fleet in Russia* is depicted in high relief. Covering a length of 22 metres, this frieze (1812, sculptor: Ivan Terebenev) plays an important visual and symbolic role in the decor of the building. Statues of ancient mythological and historical characters look down from the four corners of the parapet of the Admiralty tower.

DECEMBRISTS SQUARE

In the late 18th century, Decembrists Square was known as Peter's Square because of the monument to Peter I (the first equestrian statue in Petersburg) that was erected there in 1782. The Senate, the Synod and the Admiralty serve as the striking wings to a stage upon which the main player is the Emperor – Peter the Great. The French sculptor Etienne Falconet's most immaculate work of art was immortalised by the great Russian poet, Alexander Pushkin, in "The Bronze Horseman". Falconet's monument to Peter the Great is the centrepiece of De-

64

cembrists Square, and its striking outline is clearly visible even from afar. The monument is a sculptural symbol of an entire epoch of Russian history. It fuses the energy and many aspects of the Emperor – Creator, Reformer and Lawmaker – into one.

Peter's Square became known as Senate Square in the early 19th century due to the construction of the majestic edifice of the Senate and the Synod (1829–1836). Senate Square was rechristened in honour of a key event in the history of Russia.

63

On 14 December 1825, the ranks of demonstrators in the first organised protest for freedom, the Constitution and human rights lined up at the foot of the "Bronze Horseman". The insurgent regiments were gunned down and the uprising suppressed. The five leaders were subsequently executed and the remaining protesters permanently exiled to Siberia. The forms and symbols of Senate Square have become part of both the history and legend of Petersburg.

63. Monument to Peter the Great (*The Bronze Horseman*). 1782, sculptor: Etienne-Maurice Falconet

64. Senate and Synod. 1829–1836, architect: Carlo Rossi

65. Decembrists Square (formerly Senate Square)

ST ISAAC'S SQUARE
ST ISAAC'S CATHEDRAL

Between 1856 and 1859, under the supervision of the architect Montferrand a monument was erected to Nicholas I in the centre of St Isaac's Square. The lamps were designed by the architect Veigelt, and the low fence surrounding the pedestal was the work of Ludwig Bonshmedt. The artists Nikolai Ramazanov and Robert Zaleman took part in the creation of the sculpture, producing the somewhat naturalistic reliefs and the female figures on the pedestal. These allegorical characters, which resemble Nicholas I's wife and

66. St Isaac's Square. Monument to Nicholas I. 1856–1859, sculptor: Piotr Klodt, architect: Auguste Montferrand.
St Isaac's Cathedral. 1818–1858, architect: Auguste Montferrand

daughters, symbolise the Christian virtues: Faith (with the cross and the Gospels), Wisdom (holding a mirror), Justice (bearing the scales), and Might (with a lance and shield). The model of the equestrian statue itself was made by Piotr Klodt, who personally participated in the casting of it. The sculptor's precise mathematical calculations made it possible to use just two points of support in the mounting of the horse. The resulting sculptural group creates a striking effect when viewed from any point on the square or the neighbouring streets. The masterful execution of the central statue together with the monument's fortuitous location make it a work of genuine artistic value.

67. The miracle-working icon
of *The Tikhvin Mother of God*

68. Angels decorating the
colonnade of St Isaac's dome

69. View of the south-eastern
part of the cathedral

70. The main iconostasis

67

69

68

While St Isaac's Cathedral was under construction, the square to its south also underwent certain changes and gradually began to take on the appearance it has today. The cathedral was intended to be the greatest in the Russian Empire. Vast amounts of money and effort were required to construct this building, which stands at a height of 101.5 metres and covers over a hectare of land. It is the fourth largest domed cathedral of its type in the world after St Peter's in Rome, St Paul's in London and Santa Maria dei Fiori in Florence. Pursuant to the Greek canon, the cathedral is surmounted with a large central dome and four smaller domes at each corner. Both inside and out, the building is adorned with sculptures and reliefs.

The building that is to be seen today – the fourth to bear the name of St Isaac's – was built over the course of 40 years (1818–1858) in accordance with designs by the architect Auguste Montferrand.

71. Interior detail
of the central dome

Rectangular in shape, the body of the building has four columned porticoes, which make the vast bulk appear even larger than it already is. The interior of the cathedral (4,000 sq.m.) boasts a profusion of gilt, variegated marble, murals and mosaics. The best painters and sculptors of the time contributed to this unusual work of art.

Central to the interior decor of St Isaac's Cathedral is the combination of coloured marbles, malachite, lapis and gilt, which creates a sumptuous setting for the many magnificent sculptures, paintings and mosaics. Some of the most striking decorations

72. The chancel

73. *St Nicolas of Myra in Lycia.*
Mosaic after the original by Timofei Neff

74. Central dome

75. Chapel of St Catherine

73

74

75

are to be seen in the drum of the main dome and the area below it. A number of eminent artists and sculptors of the Academic school of the 19th century had a hand in decorating the cathedral, including Karl Briullov, Fiodor Bruni, Piotr Basin and Ivan Vitali, as well as several lesser-known masters. The mosaics inside the cathedral are particularly worthy of note. Due to the difficulty of maintaining a steady temperature within the building, it was originally planned to replace the initial paintings with mosaics. Most of the mosaics to be seen here are remarkable for their technical excellence, a fact that was celebrated at the London International Exhibition in 1862.

76. St Isaac's Cathedral. South façade

77. View of the monument to Nicholas I and the Mariinsky Palace from St Isaac's Cathedral

78

79

78. Mariinsky Palace.
1839–1844, architect:
Andrei Stackenschneider

79. Red Room

80. Timofei Neff.
*Portrait of Grand Duchess
Maria Nikolaevna.*
1850–1860

81. Palace church
of St Nicholas

THE MARIINSKY PALACE

St Isaac's Square is intersected by Bolshaya Morskaya Street. Unlike the majority of the city's main avenues, the street is not straight because it follows the bends of the Moika. By the mid-19th century, many of the existing residential buildings on Bolshaya Morskaya had been significantly renovated, and by the end of the century the district was unofficially known as "the City". In the 1840s the square was enlarged when the state purchased five houses on Bolshaya Morskaya and had them replaced with two symmetrical buildings designed by the architect Nikolai Efimov for the Ministry of State Property. St Isaac's Square also embraced the Blue Bridge, the widest in Petersburg (97.3 metres) and the former Mariinskaya Square. The appearance of the latter was dictated by the Mariinsky Palace intended as a wedding present for Nicholas I's eldest daughter, Maria. Today, the palace is occupied by the City Council.

PALACE SQUARE
THE STATE HERMITAGE

Palace Square did not gain its current title until the middle of the 18th century when the Winter Palace, the home of the Russian Emperors from 1763 to 1917, was erected along the northern edge overlooking the Neva. Today, the Winter Palace is one of five buildings that make up the architectural ensemble of the State Hermitage Museum. Catherine II ordered the construction of a new building to house her rapidly expanding collection of artworks. Thus, the Small Hermitage (1764–1775) was built onto the Winter Palace. This building, dating from the era of early Classicism, has two façades. The main façade, which looks out over the Neva, was the work of Jean-Baptiste Vallin de La Mothe. The three-

82. Palace Square.
Winter Palace.
1754–1762, architect:
Bartolomeo Francesco Rastrelli.
Alexander Column.
1834, architect:
Auguste Montferrand,
sculptor: Boris Orlovsky

83. Angel crowning the Alexander Column

83

storey wing facing Millionnaya Street was designed by Yury Velten, who linked the two parts of the building by means of a hanging garden on the first floor. Further along the embankment, beyond the Small Hermitage, stands the Old Hermitage (1771–1787), also built by Velten. The name "Old Hermitage" came about in the mid-19th century after the construction of the monumental New Hermitage (1839–1852, architect: Leo von Klenze) on the Millionnaya Street side for the growing gallery, which was finally declared a "public museum" in 1852. It is generally believed that the Hermitage was established as a museum in 1764, when Catherine II purchased a collection belonging to the merchant Johann Gotzkowsky, which included 225 canvases by renowned Western European masters. Today, the Hermitage collection, which has been put together over the course of more than two centuries, numbers about three million exhibits.

84. Winter Palace and Palace Square. Bird's-eye view

85. Fiodor Rokotov. *Portrait of Catherine II.* Late 1770s

The interiors of the Winter Palace, with rare exceptions, have not retained their original appearance: in 1837 they fell victim to a terrible fire. Nonetheless, the Winter Palace's Main Staircase (once known as the "Ambassadorial", or Jordan, Staircase), a sweeping, white marble affair with twin flights, still looks the way it did when it was installed in the 18th century. The monolithic granite columns, painted ceiling, sculptures, intricate stuccowork and abundance of gilt and mirrors make it at once festive, elegant and majestic. The St George Hall or Great Throne Room was restored by Vasily Stasov in 1842. This two-tone room with an area of 800 square metres has a distinctly august and ceremonial appearance due to the white marble columns around its perimeter and its two rows of splendid bronze chandeliers. The parquet floor is made of 16 types of wood. The Small Throne Room, or Peter the Great Hall_ is dedicated to the memory of Peter I. It was intended for small receptions. The walls of the room are covered with velvet embroidered with silver. In a large niche with a rounded vault, a gilded silver throne, made in England, stands on a raised platform. A painting depicting Peter I with the goddess Minerva hangs on the wall (1730s, Jacopo Amiconi). The décor of the Malachite Room has been preserved in its entirety. The bronze bases and capitals of the malachite columns, traced with gold, create a striking complement to the gilded doors and ceiling ornaments.

88

86. Winter Palace.
Main (Jordan) Staircase.
1754–1762, architect:
Bartolomeo Francesco
Rastrelli; 1838–1839,
architect: Vasily Stasov

87. Winter Palace.
Malachite Room.
Late 1830s – early 1840s,
architect: Alexander
Briullov

88. Winter Palace.
Peter the Great Hall
1833, architect:
Auguste Montferrand;
1842, architect:
Vasily Stasov

89

90

91

The decor of the Small Hermitage's Pavilion Hall combines elements of the Renaissance, Classical and Moorish styles. Today, the Pavilion Hall houses one of the highlights of the museum – the 18th-century Peacock Clock. In 1780, this artefact turned up in Russia, where it was bought by Prince Grigory Potemkin. The clock itself had been dismantled, and only one man – Ivan Kulibin – was able to reassemble it. This curious plaything, intended for decoration and amusement, is an intricate mechanism comprising the clockwork figures of a peacock, a cockerel, an owl and a squirrel. The dial itself is hidden in an aperture in the cap of a mushroom. When the clock is wound up, the melodious tinkling of tiny bells can be heard, after which the peacock spreads its tail feathers and the cockerel crows.

89–91. The Peacock Clock. Second half of the 18th century. England. By James Cox

92. Winter Palace. Boudoir. 1850s–1860s, architect: Harald Bosse

93. Winter Palace. Golden Drawing Room. 1839, architect: Alexander Briullov

94. Small Hermitage. Pavilion Hall. 1850–1858, architect: Andrei Stackenschneider

93

92

94

Although the Hermitage's collection of Italian paintings does not span every period of the country's rich artistic history, it is able to compete with some of the world's most famous Italian collections by virtue of the quality of the works on display and the renown of the men who created them. Particularly popular amongst visitors are Raphael's *Madonna Conestabile*, Giorgione's *Judith*, Titian's *St Sebastian*, Caravaggio's *Young Man with a Lute*, and Tintoretto's *Birth of St John the Baptist*, which are the pride of the Hermitage Museum. Without a doubt, however, two of the most outstanding and famous works to be seen here are the canvases known as *The Madonna Benois* and *The Madonna Litta*, painted by Leonardo da Vinci.

95. Old Hermitage. Leonardo da Vinci Room. 1858–1860, architect: Andrei Stackenschneider

96. Giorgione. 1478 (?)–1510. *Judith*. 1500s

97. Leonardo da Vinci. 1452–1519.
The Madonna with a Flower (The Benois Madonna). 1478

98. Leonardo da Vinci. *The Madonna Litta*. 1490

99

100

The Hermitage's collection of Dutch and Flemish art ranks amongst the greatest in the world in terms of breadth and quality. The greatest of the Dutch masters, Rembrandt Harmensz. van Rijn, is represented by 25 of his paintings, including *Flora, Danae* and *The Return of the Prodigal Son*. This priceless collection reflects all the stages of Rembrandt's sensational artistic career. The Dutch masters painted in elaborate detail, romanticising the day-to-day life of their respectable fellow countrymen without embellishing it. Works by almost all of the famous Dutch artists can be found in the Hermitage, including canvases by Adriaen van Ostade, Gerard Terborch, Willem Claesz Heda, Balthasar van der Ast, Willem Kalf, Jacob van Ruisdael, and many others. Flemish painting is notable for its extraordinary integrity. The achievements and life-affirming nature of Flemish art, which is characterised by an extensive palette and an acute sense of form and movement, are essentially summed up in the works of the leading artist of this particular school, Peter Paul Rubens. The Hermitage's collection of works by Rubens, almost all of which may be labelled masterpieces, comprises over forty work, the best of which are *The Union of Earth and Water, Perseus and Andromeda*, and *Bacchus*.

101

99. Rembrandt Harmensz
van Rijn. 1606–1669
*The Return of the Prodigal
Son.* 1668–1669

100. Winter Palace.
St George Hall
(Great Throne Room).
1795, architect: Giacomo
Quarenghi; 1842,
architect: Vasily Stasov

101. New Hermitage.
Small Skylight Room.
1842–1851, architect:
Leo von Klenze

102. Peter Paul Rubens.
1577–1640
*The Union of Earth
and Water.* c. 1618

103. Etienne Maurice
Falconet. 1716–1791
*Cupid Menacing
with His Finger.* 1758

104

The second floor of the Winter Palace houses an exhibition of the main schools of painting of the late 19th – early 20th century, Impressionism, Post-Impressionism, Fauvism and Cubism. The Hermitage's col-

105

104. Pierre-Auguste Renoir.
1841–1919
Girl with a Fan. 1881

105. Claude Monet.
1840–1926
Haystack at Giverny. 1886

106. Pablo Picasso.
1881–1973
*Woman with a Fan
(After the Ball).* 1908

107. Edgar Degas.
1834–1917
Woman Combing Her Hair.
c. 1885–1886

108. Paul Gauguin.
1848–1903
Woman Holding a Fruit.
1893

109. Henri Matisse.
1869–1954
Dance. 1910

110. Vincent van Gogh.
1853–1890
Lilac Bush. 1889

07

108

109

lighten the palette and convey impressions derived directly from everyday life without renouncing the rich artistic legacy of previous eras. Paul Cézanne, Vincent van Gogh and Paul Gauguin were also active around the time of Monet, Pissarro and Renoir. Having explored the techniques of Impressionist art, they went on to develop a new style that is commonly known as Post-Impressionism. The search for new means of expression led them to an interpretation of artistic forms that subsequently gave rise to the avant-garde art of the 20th century. Pablo Picasso and Henri Matisse, two of the greatest artists of the 20th century, are represented in the Hermitage by some of their best works. The thirty or so paintings by Picasso to be seen in the Hermitage come from a collection once belonging to Shchukin and reflect three stages in the artist's early career: the blue, pink and cubist periods. The work of Henri Matisse serves first and foremost as an assertion of the importance of colour. In each of his paintings Matisse explores the idea that "the painter must have the gift of colour, just as the singer must have a voice." He became the pioneer of a new movement known as "Fauvism" (from the French *fauves*, meaning "wild").

lection of works from this era is famed throughout the world. It is comprised largely of canvases once owned by the early 20th-century private collectors, Sergei Shchukin and Ivan Morozov, both of whom lived in Moscow. The works by Claude Monet, Camille Pissarro, Alfred Sisley and Pierre-Auguste Renoir that are to be found in the Hermitage date from the heyday of Impressionist painting. These artists discovered new ways of conveying the direct impressions created by natural phenomena. They were fascinated by the effect of light on the shape and colour of objects and its miraculous ability to change both of these factors. The Impressionists fought against the rigid traditions of classical art, seeking instead to breathe new life into painting,

110

111

112

113

111. Lekythos with a white ground *Artemis with a Swan*. Early 5th century B.C. Attica. The Pan Master

112. Gold comb *Fighting Scythians*. 4th century B.C. Solokha burial mound

113. New Hermitage. Hall of Twenty Columns. 1842–1851, architect: Leo von Klenze

114. *Venus of Tauride*. Roman copy from the original of 3rd century B.C.

115. Plaque in the shape of a deer (the Kostromskaya deer). Late 7th – early 6th century B.C. Barrow near Kostromskaya, Northern Caucasus

116. Winter Canal

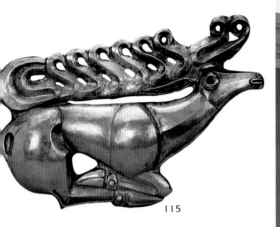

115

The ground floor of the New Hermitage houses the museum's collection of cultural and artistic relics of Ancient Greece and Rome, the Greek colonies in the Northern Black Sea and Ancient Italy. Its most valuable components include collections of Roman sculpture, antique glyptic ornaments, gold jewellery recovered from burial grounds on the north coast of the Black Sea, and a variety of Ancient Greek vases. The most striking embodiment of the antique ideal of beauty to be found in the Hermitage collection is the statue of the Tauride Venus, a Roman reproduction of a 3rd century artwork of the Hellenistic era (Greece). The Hermitage's Special Collection contains items made from precious metals by craftsmen who lived over two or three thousand years ago. Of particular interest are the

116

117

articles of Scythian culture, found during the excavation of burial mounds in the valley of the River Kuban. More specifically, these are a gold comb from the Solokha burial mound, the weighty gold *Panther* and the famous golden *Deer*, which has become one of the symbols of the Hermitage.

117. New Hermitage. Portico with Atlantes. 1848, architect: Leo von Klenze, sculptor: Alexander Terebenev

Palace Square dominates the historical centre of St Petersburg. Laid out by Carlo Rossi in 1819–1829, the square is remarkable for its harmonious blend of the monumental General Staff building, the elegant Imperial Palace, the central monolithic angel-topped granite column designed by the architect Auguste de Montferrand, and the austere building of the Guards Headquarters designed by Alexander Briullov. Palace Square is a sort of architectural centrepiece crowning the northern capital of Russia.

118. Palace Square.
General Staff building.
1819–1829, architect:
Carlo Rossi

NEVSKY PROSPEKT

Nevsky Prospekt, as straight as an arrow, is Petersburg's main street. Although it began to take shape within the first ten years of the city's existence, it developed very slowly because the attention of town planners and architects alike was centred first and foremost on the banks of the Neva and Vasilievsky Island as the intended heart of the emerging city. As a consequence of Piotr Yeropkin's famous plan to make the "trident" the basis for the layout of the city, the area between the Admiralty and the Moika became the new centre of the capital. In 1738, one of the "radial avenues" starting from the tower of the Admiralty was officially christened "Nevsky Prospekt" and declared Petersburg's main street.

12

119

121

Thenceforth, Nevsky Prospekt was the centre of much architectural activity, and over the course of the next one and a half centuries it took on the appearance it has today. The street is characterised by a sense of proportionality and integrity. Although it comprises buildings from different eras, they are all of more or less the same height. This is because of a decree issued in 1762 upon the completion of the Winter Palace, which stated that no stone buildings were to be made taller than the palace itself. On the roof of the latter stood a small tower from which signals were given to indicate that the ruling elite was departing for its country residences, and nothing was to conceal this mechanism. By the end of the 19th century,

Nevsky Prospekt had become the commercial and financial centre of bourgeois Petersburg. The appearance of the street began to change as increasing numbers of banks, offices, insurance firms and stock companies moved in. Heads of businesses sought to purchase or rent premises on the city's main thoroughfare. A splendid illustration of this is the building on the corner of Nevsky Prospekt and Griboedov Canal, the one-time home of the famous sewing machine manufacturers, Singer. This multi-storey construction of glass and metal, crowned with a globe that symbolises the spread of the company's product throughout the world, is a unique example of the architecture of the day.

124

123

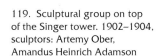

119. Sculptural group on top of the Singer tower. 1902–1904, sculptors: Artemy Ober, Amandus Heinrich Adamson

120. Singer building (House of Books). 1902–1904, architect: Pavel Suzor

121. Nevsky. White Nights...

122. Nevsky Prospekt

123. *Grand Hotel Europe* seen from the balcony of Gostiny Dvor

124. Yeliseev's shop. Detail of the roof decoration

KAZAN CATHEDRAL

The cathedral was named in honour of the holy Kazan Icon of the Mother of God, one of the precious relics of the Russian Orthodox Church that is kept there. Since the cathedral was constructed between 1801–1811, during the time of the Napoleonic campaigns, it became a unique monument to the valour of the Russian army. Field Marshal Mikhail Kutuzov, the man who led the army that defeated Napoleon in 1812, is buried inside the cathedral. The ensemble of the square is completed by two statues by Boris Orlovsky, erected in front of the cathedral in 1832. These are monuments to Field Marshals Kutuzov and Mikhail Barclay de Tolly, heroes of 1812. The colonnade that conceals the main bulk of the Cathedral of the Kazan Icon of the Mother of God lends the entire building an unusual combination of gracefulness and majesty. The elegance and august simplicity of the interior of the cathedral is also quite stunning. The best sculptors and painters were enlisted to decorate the Kazan Cathedral and transformed it into a "temple of Russian art". For several decades, the building was occupied by the Museum of Religion and Atheism. Consequently, only a few icons and precious artefacts remained within its

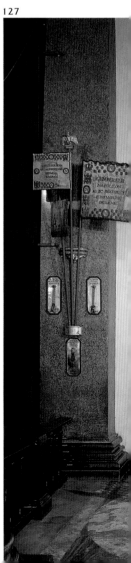

walls. Now that the cathedral has been returned to the bosom of the Church, it has once again acquired a wealth of items for use in religious ceremony.

128

129

130

125. Kazan Cathedral. 1801–1811, architect: Andrei Voronikhin

126. Monument to Field Marshal Mikhail Kutuzov. 1837, sculptor: Boris Orlovsky

127. North chapel. Tomb of Mikhail Kutuzov

128. Kazan Icon of the Mother of God

129. Interior

130. Griboyedov Canal. Bank Bridge. Griffins

PUSHKIN'S APARTMENT

A number of well-preserved private residences dating from the late 18th – early 19th century line the banks of the Moika River. Amongst them is one that is particularly dear to all Russians, for it is inseparably linked with the name of the great national poet Alexander Pushkin. Here, in the house belonging to Princess Volkonskaya, Pushkin made his final home, where he lived with his family from November 1836 until his death on 29 January 1837.

133

It is to this place that he was brought, mortally wounded, following his fatal duel with Georges d'Anthès. And it is to this place that representatives of all walks of local society thronged during Pushkin's tragic last hours, united by their grief.

131

132

134

135

136

131. Orest Kiprensky.
Portrait of Alexander Pushkin. 1827

132. Drawing room

133. Alexander Briullov.
Portrait of Natalia Pushkina. 1832

134. The poet's study

135. View of the Pushkin Memorial
Museum at 12, Moika River Embankment

136. Pushkin's watch. 1810s. Gold, silver;
chasing. Stopped at the moment
of the poet's death

137

THE RUSSIAN MUSEUM

Mikhailovskaya Street joins Nevsky Prospekt with Arts Square (formerly Mikhailovskaya Square), the product of an ingenious piece of urban design by Carlo Rossi. The architectural centrepiece of the square was the Mikhailovsky Palace, named after its owner, Grand Duke Mikhail Pavlovich, the younger brother of Alexander I.

Arts Square is a monument to the Pushkin era, the "Golden Age" of Russian culture. Hence, a statue of Pushkin was erected in the centre of the square in 1957, the work of the famous and talented sculptor Mikhail Anikushin.

In 1895, the Mikhailovsky Palace was purchased by the state to house the first state museum of national art. In conjunction with this, fundamental alterations were made to the palace interiors. Thus, only a small number of these have retained their original appearance. The Vestibule and the Main Staircase, for example, have barely changed. The most interesting room, however, is the White Hall, where not only the colourful murals, but also the furniture designed by Rossi have been preserved.

АЛЕКСАНДРУ
СЕРГЕЕВИЧУ
ПУШКИНУ

139

138

140

On 13 April 1895, Emperor Nicholas II signed Imperial Decree No. 420 "On the foundation of the special establishment called 'The Russian Museum of Emperor Alexander III' and on allotting the Mikhailovsky Palace with all its wings, services and garden for this purpose." Three years later the doors of the Mikhailovsky Palace in St Petersburg were opened to visitors to the first state museum of national fine arts in Russia. Nowaday tshe museum boasts about 400,000 exhibits – paintings, drawings, sculptures, objects of folk and applied arts. Nowadays it occupies four beautiful palaces in the centre of St Petersburg – the Mikhailovsky Palace, the Stroganov Palace, the Marble Palace and the Engineers' Castle.

137. Russian Museum (Mikhailovsky Palace). 1819–1825, architect: Carlo Rossi

138. Statue of Alexander Pushkin. 1957, sculptor: Mikhail Anikushin

139. White Hall

140. Upper landing of the Main Staircase

141

141. Unknown artist.
Portrait of Alexander III.
1880–1890

142. Karl Briullov.
1799–1852.
The Last Day of Pompeii.
1833

143. Icon: *St George and the Dragon.* 15th century

144. Large Academic Hall. 1999

145. Ivan Aivazovsky.
1817–1900.
The Tenth Wave. 1850

146. Ilya Repin.
1844–1930
The Zaporozhye Cossacks. 1880–1891

147. Vasily Surikov.
1848–1916
Taking of a Snow Fortress. 1891

148. Ivan Shishkin.
1832–1898
Mast-Tree Grove. 1898

The Russian Museum has lately accumulated a significant collection of early Russian artworks. These include such priceless icons as *The Angel with the Golden Hair* and S*t George and the Dragon.* The museum officially opened in 1895. At the time, it contained 445 paintings, which were taken from the Academy of Arts Museum, the Hermitage and other palace collections. Thus, the Hermitage contributed the world-famous illustration of *The Last Day of Pompeii* by Karl Briullov, the huge canvas depicting *The Brazen Serpent* by Fiodor Bruni, and Ivan Aivazovsky's most

celebrated seascape, *The Tenth Wave.* These works were to be seen in the large rooms devoted to Academic painting. An entire series of splendid large-scale portraits by Karl Briullov, otherwise known as "the great Karl", hangs in the Russian Museum. Gogol once wrote that, "his works are the first to have the enviable fate of enjoying world-wide acclaim, and the most highly reputed of these to this day is *The Last Day of Pompeii*". The gems of the exhibit included canvases by Ivan Kramskoy, Nikolai Gay, Ivan Shishkin, Nikolai Yarochenko, Vasily Surikov and Mikhail Vrubel. One of the most popular figures among the

143

142

144

145

146

147

148

149

151

150

The museum owns the world's best collection of works by the Russian avant-garde artists, including such internationally acclaimed painters as Wassily Kandinsky, Kasimir Malevich and Pavel Filonov. Kandinsky was the founder of abstract painting, the first to find new ways of expressing the spiritual side of human existence and of liberating art from the study of objects by exploring the vibrancy and expressiveness of colour and rhythm. Filonov developed his own technique of "analytical art". His works organically combine the objective and the subjective, the rational and the intuitive. The objective world, when subjected

Russian artists of the late 19th – early 20th century was Ilya Repin. His art is represented in the Russian Museum by many works from various periods beginning with his earliest essays as an artist. One of the greatest achievements of his artistic career is the picture *The Zaporozhye Cossacks*, painted between 1880 and 1891.

152

154

155

156

to the analysis of the brush, is transformed into a picture of the universal, of that which is conceived by the energy of the Creator. Malevich, having studied Impressionism and Cubism, completed the transition to formlessness by "inventing" Suprematism – a variety of geometric abstraction. Supre-matism, in the artist's own words, can be divided into three stages represented by an equal number of squares, black, red and white. "The basis for their construction was an essential economical principle, i.e., to convey the power of statics or of visible, dynamic peace in one dimension."

149. Nikolai Roerich.
1874–1947
Guests from Overseas.
1902

150. Marc Chagall.
1887–1985
Promenade. 1917

151. Zinaida Serebriakova.
1884–1967
In a Bath-House. 1913

152. Pavel Kuznetsov.
1878–1968
Shearing Sheep

153. Boris Kustodiev.
1878–1927
Merchant's Wife At Tea.
1918

154. Kasimir Malevich.
1878–1935
Red Cavalry. 1918

155. Kasimir Malevich.
1878–1935
Portrait of a Woman.
c. 1930

156. Liubov Popova.
1889–1924
Man+Air+Space

157. Wassily Kandinsky.
1866–1944
Twilight. 1917

157

158

OSTROVSKY SQUARE AND YELISEEV'S SHOP

The entire architectural ensemble of Ostrovsky Square, which opens out onto Nevsky Prospekt, and the street that links it to another smaller plaza now known as Lomonosov Square, became one of Rossi's greatest masterpieces of urban design.

The humble task of building the Alexandrinsky Theatre evolved into a fantastic plan to create an entire block. To begin with, two small pavilions (1817–1818), linked by a beautiful fence, appeared on the eastern side of the square. They served as the arsenal of the Anichkov Palace (1741–1750s), a building that a number of architects had a hand in, including Rastrelli. The palace was built for Elizabeth Petrovna, who presented it to her favourite and, as legend has it, morganatic husband, Count Alexei Razumovsky. Before the October Revolution of 1917, it was the site of one of the imperial residences.

The main component of the Ostrovsky Square ensemble, the Alexandrinsky Theatre, was erected in 1832, and is now an outstanding monument to Russian Classicism.

In 1873, a monument to Catherine II was erected in the centre of the square. At the feet of the towering Empress sit eminent figures of her time, including dignitaries, military leaders, scientists and artists.

158. Monument to Catherine II. 1873, designed by Mikhail Mikeshin, sculptors: Alexander Opekushin, Matvei Chizhov

159. Architect Rossi Street

160. Alexandrinsky Theatre. 1828–1832, architect: Carlo Rossi

161. Yeliseev's shop. 1902–1903, architect: Gavriil Baranovsky

162. View of Ostrovsky Square from the chariot atop the Alexandrinsky Theatre

Yeliseev's emporium belonged to one of the representatives of a famous dynasty of merchants. Today, the building that houses the shop is also the home of the Akimov Comedy Theatre.

161

162

164

THE ANICHKOV BRIDGE

Built at Peter I's behest in 1715, the Anichkov Bridge was one of the first bridges in Petersburg. The principal feature of the bridge is the sculptural ensemble known as "The Taming of the Horse". It was the sculptor himself who suggested that the statues be placed on the Anichkov Bridge. Only two components of the original bronze sculptural group (1841) were installed: the remaining figures, facing Liteiny Prospekt, were substituted with painted plaster models since, by order of Nicholas I, the bronze originals were sent to Berlin as a gift for the king of Prussia. When the sculptor cast a second set in bronze, these too were sent abroad, this time to Naples. Later, in 1848, Klodt created two new groups, different to their predecessors, for the vacant pedestals on the bridge.

165

166

163, 165. Anichkov
Bridge. 1785,
engineers: Johann
Gerard, Piotr Sukhtelen;
1841, engineer:
Ivan Butats; architect:
Alexander Briullov
(railings)

164. Sculptural group:
The Taming of the Horse
1841–1850, sculptor:
Piotr Klodt

166. Beloselsky-
Belozersky Palace.
1847–1848, architect:
Andrei Stackenschneider

167. Main Staircase

168, 169. Gold Drawing
Room

167

169

168

THE BELOSELSKY-
BELOZERSKY PALACE

On the corner of Nevsky and the Fontanka stands the Beloselsky-Belozersky Palace, which was fundamentally redesigned by Andrei Stackenschneider in 1847–1848 "in the style of Rastrelli". The palace's first owner was Prince Alexander Beloselsky-Belozersky, a member of a family line leading back to the Kievan princes and the princes Beloselskie, who earned a name for themselves in the service of Peter I. Today, the Beloselsky-Belozersky Palace is the home of the City Cultural Centre. This organisation strives to preserve the artistic atmosphere that once prevailed within the building's walls.

170

171

172

170. Panoramic view
of the Field of Mars

171. Bird's eye view
of the city centre

172. Monument to
Generalissimo Alexander
Suvorov. 1801, sculptor:
Mikhail Kozlovsky

THE FIELD OF MARS

In the second half of the 18th century, during the reign of Paul I, a military parade ground known as the Field of Mars was founded on Poteshny Meadow, once the site of public fetes, splendid firework displays and a large public theatre. The Field of Mars stretched for 500 metres from north to south and 300 metres from east to west.

It was a huge open space that was snow-covered in winter and dusty in the summer, hence its nickname the "Petersburg Sahara". The square on the Field of Mars itself came into being in 1924 after participants in the February Revolution of 1917 were buried there and a monument (the work of the architect Lev Rudnev) was erected over the graves. In the 1930s, the place was transformed into a park.

THE CHURCH ON THE SPILLED BLOOD (CHURCH OF THE RESURRECTION)

The Church on the Spilled Blood is both an historical monument and a work of art. The men who built it were given the difficult task of incorporating the spot on which the tragic attempt upon the life of Emperor Alexander II was committed into the interior of the church. The site of the murder is marked by a special chapel in the western part of the building beneath the bell. Here, in an area slightly below floor-level, part of the carriageway and railings that were stained with blood at the time of the assassination can be seen. The specific conditions for the construction of the church are the reason for another of the building's idiosyncrasies: it has no central entrance. Instead, on either side of the bell-tower is a parvis with its own doorway. Inside the Church on the Spilled Blood there is not a single painting: the walls are almost entirely covered with mosaics. Although the love of the faithful did not save the church from being closed in 1930, the will of God saved it from destruction during the Blockade when a shell fell on a cupola but

173. Church on the Spilled Blood (Church of the Resurrection). 1883–1907, architects: Alfred Parland, Archimandrite Ignaty (Ignaty Malyshev)

174. Cupolas of the church

175. *The Crucifixion of Christ*. Mosaic in the lower part of the bell tower. Designed by Alfred Parland

176. Central nave and the canopy

177. Interior of the church viewed from the canopy

178. Egor Botman. *Portrait of Alexander II.* 1856

176

177

178

179. *Christ
the Pantocrator.*
Mosaic in the central
dome. Designed by
Nikolai Kharlamov

180. *Holy Martyr Alexandra the Empress.*
St Mary Magdalene. Mosaics in the iconostasis.
Designed by Nikolai Bodarevsky

181. *The Calling of Matthew.*
Mosaic on the north wall.
Designed by Andrei Riabushkin

did not explode. The building was further preserved by the bravery of the sappers who risked their lives in 1961 to defuse the missile. The skill and truly selfless efforts of the restorers, engineers, architects, technicians and everyone who worked on the restoration of the church have made it possible for this wonderful and unique edifice to once more bask in its own splendour and delight and amaze all who see it.

The construction of the church and work on the decor took 24 years (1883–1907). The church is 81 metres high with a total area of 1,642 square metres. Stone-cutters, artists, mosaicists, ceramists and enamellers were involved in the creation of its striking artistic ornaments. The outside of the church is decorated largely with mosaics, while the cupolas are covered with bright enamels and the hipped roofs with coloured tiles. Together they make up a unique collection, which has no equal anywhere else in the world. The 308 mosaics, with a total area of 6,560 square metres,

are a true artistic and cultural treasure. Besides traditional iconographic subjects, the coats of arms of Russian cities and administrative units are also depicted in the mosaics that cover three sides of the bell-tower. The mosaics were prepared by both Russian experts and a number of foreign firms. Sketches for the mosaics were made by a group of over 25 artists. Forty-two of the mosaics are the work of Nikolai Kharlamov, including *The Pantocrator* on the plafond of the central dome, which is one of the artist's most memorable works. *The Eucharist* is a liturgical interpretation of the Last Supper, depicting the sacred idea of the establishment of the rite of Communion, rather than an historical portrayal showing Christ's prediction of His imminent betrayal by Judas. In *The Eucharist*, the Saviour offers His disciples the holy bread with His right hand ("Take, this is my body"), while with His left He gives them the cup of wine ("This is my blood of the covenant, which is poured out for many").

182. *The Eucharist*. Designed by Nikolai Kharlamov

183. The main iconostasis

183

184

lomeo Rastrelli, father of the renowned architect. In its day, the model for this sculpture was approved by Peter the Great himself, yet the path to the realisation of the sculptor's plans and the raising of the monument was a long one.

186

THE MIKHAILOVSKY CASTLE

The Mikhailovsky Castle was built on the site of the wooden Summer Palace of Elizabeth Petrovna. By design, the building constitutes a square with an octagonal courtyard in the middle. The castle was named after the church within its walls, which was dedicated to the Archangel Michael, the dread leader of the heavenly host. The building's appearance is a reflection of its owner's darkly romantic imagination. The castle was surrounded by a moat, which was passable only by means of drawbridges.

The castle served as the imperial residence for only 40 days. In 1823, it was taken over by the Engineering Academy and acquired its second name, the "Engineer's Castle". From 1837 to 1842, Fiodor Dostoevsky was educated here. One of the most "Petersburg" writers, he disliked the city and its founder intensely and refused to acknowledge "Peter's doings" as the Europeanisation of Russia. In front of the castle, on the parade ground, stands a monument to Peter the Victor, the work of Carlo Barto-

185

87

188

184. Panoramic view of St Petersburg from the roof of the Mikhailovsky Castle

185. Mikhailovsky Castle. 1784–1800, architects: Vasily Bazhenov, Vincenzo Brenna

186. Stepan Shchukin. *Portrait of Paul I.* 1800

187. South façade

188. Monument to Peter the Great. 1800, sculptor: Bartolomeo Carlo Rastrelli

189. Church of the Archangel Michael. Iconostasis

190

THE SUMMER GARDENS

The oldest gardens in Petersburg are the Summer Gardens, which are one of the most magnificent and unique monuments to 18th-century park culture. Laid out in 1704, they initially stretched from the Neva to what would eventually become Nevsky Prospekt. Gradually, however, as the city expanded and the value of land in the city centre increased, a substantial part of this territory was occupied by new buildings.

192

The Summer Gardens were envisaged as a "regular garden" of the Baroque era. The remaining statues in the Summer Gardens (there were 220, of which 91 have survived) were created by Italian sculptors at the beginning of the 18th century.

The "best railing in the world" was erected along the northern edge of the garden, separating it from the thoroughfare along

94

193

194

195

190. Panoramic view
of the Summer Gardens
from the roof of the
Mikhailovsky Castle

191. Statue of Ceres.
Late 17th century,
sculptor: Thomas
Quellinus

192. Railings around
the Summer Gardens.
1771–1784, architects:
Yuri Velten, Piotr Egorov

193. An alley in the
gardens

194. Peter I's Summer
Palace. 1711–1712,
architects: Andreas
Schlüter, Domenico
Trezzini

195. Peter I's Bedroom

196. *Peace and
Abundance*. 1722,
sculptor: Pietro Baratta

the Palace Embankment. In 1711–1712,
in the northeastern corner of the gardens,
Peter I's Summer Palace was built, which,
contrary to the traditions of park design,
did not constitute the centrepiece of the
composition. This modest house, a two-
storey building with a high roof, hardly
conforms to the idea of a palace fit for the
"founder of the sovereign state".

196

197

198

200

197. Stefano Torelli.
Portrait of Grigory Orlov.
After 1763

198. View of the Palace
Embankment

199. Marble Palace.
1768–1785, architect:
Antonio Rinaldi

200. Main Staircase

201. Marble Hall

202. Valentin Serov.
*Portrait of Zinaida
Yusupova.* 1902

203. Yusupov Palace.
1830–1838, architect:
Andrei Mikhailov

204. Grigory Rasputin

205. Princess's Boudoir

206. Auditorium
of the Home Theatre

THE MARBLE PALACE

The earliest of the grand-ducal buildings on the Palace Embankment is the Marble Palace. The only residence not to be named after its owner, it is a unique monument to decorative art. The façade of the first and second floors of the palace are clad in marble of various shades from all over the world. The palace interiors were also decorated with marble, but only the main staircase and the lower tier of the large hall have survived. Although the marble has faded and lost its brilliance due to the local climate, the palace is rightfully regarded as a gem of early Russian Classical architecture. The palace was first owned by Grigory Orlov, a favourite of Catherine II who presented him with this token of her "gratitude". The palace now belongs to the Russian Museum. In the courtyard stands a statue of Alexander III astride a horse. This work by Paolo Trubetsky was located in the centre of the square near the Moscow Railway Station until 1936.

199

201

202

203

THE YUSUPOV PALACE

The most famous residence on the Moika is the Yusupov Palace. Here, on the night of 16 December 1916, Grigory Rasputin was murdered in a prologue to the revolutionary events of 1917. In the eyes of Nicholas II and his wife Alexandra Fiodorovna, the Siberian peasant, seer and miracle worker embodied a mystic link between the Orthodox tsar and the people. Having lost the support of the upper echelons of society, the Russian autocrat hoped to curry favour with the common people with the aid of this man. Rasputin himself was aware that he was the royal family's last hope not only to stay on the throne, but also, with his apparent psychic powers, to preserve the health of the heir apparent, who suffered from haemophilia. Vexed by Rasputin's influence over the tsar, aristocrats and representatives of the royal circles alike felt compelled to take extreme measures. A conspiracy arose, and members of distinguished families finally sought to assassinate the "holy man". In the palace basement is the room to which Felix Yusupov lured Rasputin in order to implement their brutal plan. Legend has it that neither poisoned cakes, nor two shots from a revolver, nor a fierce blow to the head were sufficient to kill him. It was not until Rasputin was thrown into the river that he finally died.

204

205

206

207

209

207. Mariinsky Theatre
1847–1849, 1859,
architect: Albert Kavos;
1883–1886, 1894,
architect: Viktor Shroeter

208. *Prince Igor*
by Alexander Borodin
at the Mariinsky Theatre

209, 213. Auditorium

210. *Sleeping Beauty*
by Piotr Tchaikovsky

211. Anna Pavlova
in *Chopiniana* by Frederic
Chopin. 1907

212. Galina Ulanova
in *Giselle* by Adolph Adam.
1940

THE MARIINSKY THEATRE

The Mariinsky Theatre opened its first season on 2 October 1860 with Mikhail Glinka's opera *A Life for the Tsar*. Music by the famous Russian composers Nikolai Rimsky-Korsakov, Modest Mussorgsky and Piotr Tchaikovsky would be heard for the first time within its walls. The Mariinsky hosted productions by Marius Petipa. The dancers Mathilda Kshesinskaya, Anna Pavlova, Tamara Karsavina, Vatslav Nijinsky and Mikhail Fokin brought these spectacles great acclaim. The Russian school of opera also developed in the Mariinsky. Leading roles were performed by Leonid Sobinov and Fiodor Chaliapin. During this period, the scenery for many of the productions was created by the

208

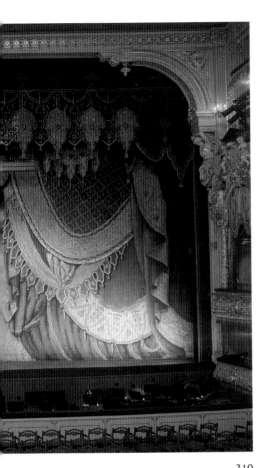

artists Alexander Benois, Konstantin Korovin and Alexander Golovin, who, in 1914, designed the stage curtain that hangs in the theatre to this day. In the early 20th century, many of the Mariinksy's soloists starred in Serguei Diaghilev's "Russian Seasons". It is here that Galina Ulanova embarked upon her artistic career.

With the coming of the famous musician Valery Gerguiev, many interesting experimental productions began to be staged, testifying to a relentless search for innovative forms in the fields of opera and ballet as well as the art of set design. The traditions of the famous stage and the rich history of expertise are painstakingly upheld within the theatre's walls.

211

212

210

213

THE ST NICHOLAS CATHEDRAL

The area of town in which the St Nicholas Cathedral, or "Sailor's Church", stands today was once occupied by quarters for members of the Naval Department. The first service was held in the St Nicholas Cathedral on 14 September 1770, following the defeat of the Turkish armada at Chesma Bay. Following the Russian tradition, there are two churches in the cathedral. The upper, Theophany Church is used mainly on Sundays and on the days of religious feasts and has a brighter, airy feel and a typically Baroque exuberance. The lower (winter) church, intended for daily use, is lit by icon lamps, candles and chandeliers, creating a magical effect. Thus, the pale blue and gold two-storey edifice with its five domes is a splendid sight both inside and out. The interior of the church is richly decorated with gilt carving, particularly fine examples of which are to be seen on the iconostasis dating from 1755–1760. Sculptures and columns wreathed with carved garlands also feature heavily in the design of the icon screen. An icon of St Nicholas, one of the most popular saints in Russia, where he is known as "Nicholas the Miracle Worker", is to be found inside the St Nicholas Cathedral. Nicholas is regarded as the saint who is "swift to aid". He is always depicted on icons as a balding old man dressed in robes that indicate his venerable status as a clergyman. His figure is typically shown full-length with his right hand raised in blessing and his left holding the Gospels. An important part of the architectural ensemble of the St Nicholas Cathedral is the freestanding four-tiered belfry, which with its beautiful lines ranks amongst the most sublime works of Russian architecture.

214. Interior of the
Upper (Theophany)
Church

215. View of the
St Nicholas Cathedral
grounds

216. St Nicholas
Cathedral. 1753–1762,
architect: Savva
Chevakinsky

217. Icon: *St Nicholas
the Miracle Worker*

216

217

218

THE ST ALEXANDER NEVSKY MONASTERY

Founded by order of Peter I in 1710, the St Alexander Nevsky Monastery is almost as old as the city itself. It was named in honour of St Alexander Nevsky, an outstanding 13th-century holy prince and statesman who was declared patron saint of St Petersburg by the Orthodox Church. Under his command, the Russian army triumphed over the Swedes on the banks of the Neva in 1240. Peter I decided to transfer the relics of the Orthodox Russian warrior to the new capital and thus work began on the urgent construction of the St Alexander Nevsky Monastery. In 1797, it was declared a *lavra*, the term used to describe

218. St Alexander Nevsky Monastery. Entrance

219. Tchaikovsky's tomb. 1897, sculptor: Piotr Kamensky

220. Dostoevsky's grave. 1883, sculptor: Nikolai Laveretsky

219

220

the most important Orthodox monasteries. Within the walls of the monastery, on either side of the main entrance, lies a pair of cemeteries. Many Russian writers, artists, composers and performers are buried here.

221

223

22

224

221. Holy Trinity
Cathedral. 1776–1790,
architect: Ivan Starov

222. Central nave

223. Shrine containing
the relics of Saint
Alexander Nevsky

224. Inner courtyard
of the monastery

THE HOLY TRINITY CATHEDRAL

Throughout the 18th century, many famous architects worked on the monastery, transforming it into an architectural ensemble that comprised buildings of different eras and styles. The construction of the monastery was completed by the renowned Russian architect Ivan Starov. He created the majestic Holy Trinity Cathedral, which plays an important symbolic and compositional role in the monastery ensemble. The cathedral, which boasts two monumental belfries, is an example of religious architecture in the style of late 18th-century Russian Classicism. The gilded bronze gates of the iconostasis are of remarkable elegance and beauty.

225

22

225. Cathedral of the Transfiguration. 1743–1754, architects: Mikhail Zemtsov, Pietro Trezzini; 1828–1829, architect: Vasily Stasov

226. Religious procession. Patriarch Alexis II

227. Cathedral of the Transfiguration. Image Not-Made-By-Hands of Our Lord Jesus Christ

228. Church of the Vladimir Icon of the Mother of God. 1761–1769. Belfry. 1783, architect: Giacomo Quarenghi

229. Chesme Church of the Nativity of St John the Baptist. 1777–1780, architect: Yuri Velten

22

ST PETERSBURG CHURCHES

Having ascended the throne, Peter I abolished the patriarchate and during the Petersburg era of Russian history, the Orthodox Church practically became a state organ. One of the signs of the Church's subordination to the state was the consecration of churches in the name of "calendar saints" who shared the names of Emperors, or in honour of saints, whose days coincided with the dates of events that were significant to the state, such as a military victory. The defeat of the Turks at Chesma Bay in 1770 was marked by the founding of the Church of the Nativity of St John the Baptist, better known as the Chesma Church. The Convent of St John of Kronstadt on the Karpovka River serves as a reminder of the saint who established this very institution. At the beginning of 1917 there were over 700 churches and chapels in Petersburg. Now there are approximately 100. A number of these religious buildings have now been handed back to the Church and, thanks to the efforts of restorers, their interiors have been recreated.

THE SMOLNY MONASTERY

The palaces and residences built in the Baroque style by the court architect Bartolomeo Francesco Rastrelli adorn the city to this day. One such work is the ensemble of the Smolny Convent situated on the upper left-hand bank of the Neva at a bend in the river. After Peter had conquered this territory, a large tar yard was built. Later, a country palace was erected here for Elizabeth and christened "Smolny" (meaning *tar*). Legend has it that in the fourth year of her reign, Elizabeth intended to hand the reins of government to her nephew, Peter III, and end her days peacefully in a convent. Cherishing this thought, she ordered the construction of a religious retreat for women on the spot where her palace stood, to be named the Convent of the Resurrection. The plans and construction work were entrusted to Rastrelli. All of the convent buildings are laid out symmetrically. In the centre stands the lofty cathedral, while around the edge of the courtyard run the living quarters with small "domestic" churches at each corner.

The Cathedral of the Resurrection in the Smolny Convent looks particularly striking both from the water and from the opposite bank.

232

230. Smolny Cathedral.
1748–1769, architect:
Bartolomeo Francesco
Rastrelli

231. View of the
Smolny Monastery and
Bolsheokhtinsky Bridge

232. Panoramic view
of the monastery

233

234

235

233. Smolny Institute. 1806–1808, architect: Giacomo Quarenghi. Statue of Lenin. 1927, sculptor: Vasily Kozlov, architect: Vladimir Shchuko

234. Vladimir Serov. *Winter Palace is Taken by Storm.* 1954

235. The cruiser *Aurora* at permanent anchor

236. Smolny Propylaea. 1923–1924, architects: Vladimir Shchuko, Vladimir Helfreich

237. Vladimir Serov. *Lenin proclaiming the power of the Soviets.* 1936

THE GREAT OCTOBER REVOLUTION

In August 1917, the Petrograd Soviet of Workers' and Soldiers' Deputies moved into the former Smolny Institute for Young Noblewomen. In September, leadership in the Soviets passed to the Bolshevik Party and Leon Trotsky was elected its chairman. Whereas the Provisional Government and the Soviets had previously worked towards a common goal, namely, the creation of a democratic Russian government, the Petrograd Soviet now assumed a very different stance, setting its sights on an armed uprising. It identified its goal as "proletarian dictatorship" and adopted the slogan: "All power to the Soviets." Power was to be accepted by the second All-Russian Congress of Soviets. At the sound of a shot fired from the battleship *Aurora*, soldiers, sailors and Red Guards stormed the Winter Palace and arrested the Provisional Government. Lenin announced to the delegates of the Congress gathered in the assembly hall at the Smolny that all power in Russia was now in their hands. The second All-Russian Congress of Soviets of Workers' and Soldiers' Deputies elected the Soviet government. For many years, the Smolny was regarded as the bastion and symbol of Soviet power.

THE SIEGE OF LENINGRAD

During the Second World War Leningrad lived through the most tragic episode in its existence, the 900-day siege lasting from September 1941 to January 1944. In 1941, German troops were stopped short just outside Leningrad. A division of militiamen, citizen soldiers who were badly armed and hastily trained, played a vital role in defending the city, resolving to protect it at the cost of their own lives. Although the enemy did not enter the city, Leningrad was cut off from the rest of the country and the most horrific siege in the history of man began. Weakened by hunger, numbed by fierce frosts and deprived of electricity and water, people struggled to defend their native land and, with energy and resoluteness, fought for survival in the vast city. In winter, Leningrad was supplied with food and munitions by the Road of Life. This was

238

238, 239, 241.
Monument to the Heroic
Defenders of Leningrad
on Victory Square.
1974–1975, architect:
Sergei Speransky,
sculptor: Mikhail
Anikushin

240. Piskarevskoe
Memorial Cemetery.
Statue of the Motherland.
1956–1960, sculptor:
Vera Isaeva; architects:
Alexander Vasiliev,
Evgueny Levinson

242. Patrol on the streets
of Leningrad

243. At a water pump
on Nevsky Prospekt

239

240

241

242

243

the name given to the route, 100 kilometres long, which linked the city with the Osinovets Cape on Lake Ladoga and, when the lake was frozen, with its eastern shore. The uninterrupted activity of this legendary route was maintained at the cost of the lives of numerous drivers, sappers, railwaymen, soldiers, pilots, anti-aircraft gunners, and artillery men.

In January 1943, the blockade was broken on a narrow strip of the front. A monument to the courage and fortitude of the citizens of Leningrad stands at the Piskarevskoe Memorial Cemetery. Buried here are about 450 thousand persons who perished during the siege. Over one million people died in Leningrad during the war – civilians and soldiers alike. About twenty thousand persons were killed in air raids.

THE BRIDGES OF ST PETERSBURG

During Peter's reign, there were no bridges over the Neva. The Emperor wanted the people of Petersburg, to their dismay, to share his passion for sailing, thus riverboats were the common form of transport. Peter even made it a tradition to take his retinue out in rowing- and sailing boats. Many members of his circle set out on these excursions praying to holy icons in dread of the perfidious waters. It was not until after the death of the autocrat and "sailor" that three floating bridges appeared across the Neva. These were dismantled at the time of the spring thaws and the late autumn freezes. Only in the mid-19th century were they finally replaced with permanent bridges made of metal. Each of Petersburg's bridges has its own distinctive structure and appearance. They are humpbacked and elegant, large and small, subtle and

2

imposing. Their decorative wrought iron railings and lamps, coupled with the granite embankments, give the face of the city a charming and inimitable look. At either end of the small pedestrian Lion Bridge sit two pairs of enormous lions (2.23 metres high). In their half open jaws they hold the wrought iron rings and thick steel cables that support this striking suspension bridge.

244. Griboyedov Canal.
Bank Bridge. 1825–1826,
engineer: Wilhelm Traitteur,
sculptor: Pavel Sokolov

245. Griboyedov Canal.
Italian Bridge. 1955,
engineer: A. Gutsait,
architect V. Vasilkovsky

246. Moika River
Embankment

247. Panoramic view
of the Moika River
and Kriukov Canal

248. Griboyedov Canal.
Lion Bridge. 1825–1826,
engineer: Wilhelm Traitteur,
sculptor: Pavel Sokolov

249

WHITE NIGHTS

The unpredictability of the elements makes Petersburg a profoundly expressive city. It has the ability to change its countenance unexpectedly, compelling us to see its beauty in a new light. It is as if the city senses the mood of its inhabitants and seeks to share with them both their joy and melancholy, but the famous White Nights seem almost to compensate for the frequent rains, clammy mists, short winter days and long autumn nights.

251

250

The best part of the year is widely considered to be the period from May to June known as the "White Nights", when as many people are out and about during the night as during the day, with an even greater number than usual strolling along the embankments. Music and laughter are heard everywhere as people while away the hours in countless restaurants and cafes, go for boat rides along the rivers and canals, or simply enjoy the spectacle of the

252

253

249. White Nights festival

250. View of the Trinity Bridge and Peter and Paul Fortress from the Kutuzov Embankment

251. White Nights. View of the Neva from the roof of the Winter Palace

252, 254. Palace Bridge opening

253. Lieutenant Schmidt Bridge

bridges – for the sight of the steel spans rearing up to allow ships to pass through is a truly unforgettable spectacle. City residents have to put up with a certain amount of inconvenience, adjusting their movements across the Neva to the bridge-opening timetable; yet they also traditionally take pride in this uniquely Petersburgian phenomenon. The White Nights are also the season of special cultural events: arts festivals including classical music, jazz, rock music and cinema; and the school-leaving balls that for generations have marked young people's coming of age.

"A multitude of poets have extolled and described our northern nights, but to express their beauty in words is as

impossible as describing the scent of a rose and the tremor of a string fading into air. No poet can convey the inexpressible, mysterious silence, pregnant with thoughts and life, that rests on the heavily respiring Neva after the heat of day in the phosphorescent light of the frail clouds and crimson west. No painter can capture the wondrous shades and hues that play in the sky and are reflected in the rivers as on the skin of a chameleon, in the facets of crystal or the polarisation of light. No musician can transpose into earthly tongues the sounds, permeated with feeling, that rise up from the earth to the skies only to fall back to earth once more reflected by the heavens" (Apollon Grigoriev).

255. View of the Great
Palace and Grand Cascade

256. Grand Cascade.
Fountain: *Samson
Tearing Open the Jaws
of the Lion.* 1801,
sculptor: Mikhail
Kozlovsky; architect:
Andrei Voronikhin;
cast by Vasily Ekimov

256

PETERHOF

No description of St Petersburg would be complete without some mention of the former imperial residences that are strung out around the edges of the northern capital like the beads of an exquisite necklace. Many of these park and palace complexes came into being at the same time as the city and, in accordance with Peter I's plans, became a delightful and fitting frame for Petersburg. The most deserving of our attention is Peterhof, the favourite residence of Peter I, after whom it is named. Peterhof constitutes a grandiose 18th–19th century architectural and park ensemble with an area of over a thousand

257

257. Decorative sculpture

258. *Perseus.* 1801, sculptor: Feodossy Shchedrin

259. *Wounded Amazon.* 1801, sculptor: Fiodor Gordeev. Copy of an original 5th–4th century B.C.

258

259

hectares dotted with approximately thirty buildings and pavilions and decorated with over one hundred sculptures.

15 August 1723 saw the official opening of Peterhof. The arrangement of fountains on the terraces and in the lower park was developed and a gravity-fed water system installed in the Petrine era. At the time, these unique ornaments were given

261

260

different shapes and sizes in order to achieve an array of effects with the falling water. By skilfully exploiting the lay of the extensive territory with its natural ledges, slopes and plains, architects, engineers and sculptors succeeded in creating a picturesque park and peerless architectural ensemble. In front of the northern façade of the palace, stretching down towards the sea, is the Lower Park, which embraces a variety of buildings and numerous fountains. At the centre of this magnificent symmetrical composition is the Grand Cascade. Besides the fountains themselves, sculptures and bas-reliefs play an important symbolic and ornamental part in the Grand Cascade ensemble. In the form of allegories, they represent and celebrate Russia's military prowess and naval might. The centrepiece of the Cascade is the fountain of *Samson Tearing Open the Jaws of the Lion*, which was created in honour of the 25th anniversary of an important Russian victory. On 27 June 1709, St Samson's Day, the famous Poltava Battle took place in which the Russian army, led by Peter I, routed King Charles XII of Sweden's troops. The aforesaid sculpture was to serve as an allegorical expression of Russia's triumph, a task that naturally dictated the monument's design.

260. West staircase

261. View of the Grand Canal (otherwise known as the Sea or Samson Canal)

262. *Galatea*. 1801, sculptor: Jean-Dominique Rachette

262

263

264

26

263. Great Palace. Main Staircase

264, 265. Main Staircase. Upper landing

266. Ballroom

267. Throne Room

The Great Palace is the main building of the Peterhof ensemble. The staterooms and drawing rooms are located on the first floor. Rastrelli made the largest of these the Throne Room, which has an area of 300 metres. A double row of windows in the Ballroom reflected in a series of mirrors visually increases the size of the hall. A large number of windows of different shapes and sizes interspersed with strategically placed mirrors were a common device used in Baroque architecture to create the illusion of endless space. In the Petrine era the Portrait Hall was also the largest room. The big, two-tone hall in the very centre of the palace has windows and doors on two sides. To the south the Upper Park is to be seen, while to the north lie the Grand Cascade and the gulf in all their glory.

268

268. Roman Fountain.
1738–1739; 1799–1800

269. Eve Fountain.
1718, sculptor:
Giovanni Bonazza
1725–1726, architect:
Niccolo Michetti

269

The Grand Cascade divides the Lower Park into east and west, each side having its own smaller cascade. In the eastern area of the park, the Chessboard Hill or Dragon Cascade adorns a natural incline. At its head, three fantastic winged dragons spit water from between their fanged jaws,

270

271

272

273

which flows down a chequered slope. Both sides of the cascade are decorated with marble statues made by early 18th-century Italian masters. In front of the Chessboard Hill stand two Roman Fountains, which were created in the first half of the 18th century. They were originally made of wood, but were refashioned in marble at the end of the century. They resemble the two-tiered fountains on the square in front of St Peter's Cathedral in Rome.

The Pyramid Fountain is completely different by design with its granite pedestal sat on three marble steps. This water obelisk is an impressive sight: seven tiers of foaming jets spring from over five hundred concealed apertures. Together with such monumental ornaments, the park also contains smaller, elegant fountains such as The Sun. The sound of the latter's murmuring streams is reminiscent of an intimate conversation, while the scattered sprays of its central jet lit up by varicoloured lights give the fountain its name. Each of the ornamental fountains in the grounds is the "hero" of a particular subject. The Adam and Eve fountains remind visitors that they are in a veritable

earthly paradise. "The Favourite" is an illustration of La Fontaine's fable about a dog trying to catch ducks. Peterhof is famed largely for its fountains, which are both ingenious works of hydraulic engineering and masterpieces of monumental decorative art. The glittering, iridescent jets of the three cascades and the many fountains playing in the rays of the sun create the unique sensation of a celebration of nature and the apotheosis of Peter the Great's own favourite element – water. The variety of forms and the different functions played

270. Sun Fountain. 1721–1724, architect: Niccolo Michetti

271. Pyramid Fountain. 1721–1724, architect: Mikhail Zemtsov

272. Mushroom Fountain. 1735, sculptor: Carlo Bartolomeo Rastrelli; engineer: Paul Sualem

273. Wheatsheaf Fountain. 1721–1723, architect: Niccolo Michetti. Designed by Peter I

274

274. View of the
Seafront Terrace and
the Monplaisir Palace

275. Monplaisir Garden.
Bell Fountain. *Psyche.*
1817. Copy of the
original by Antonio
Canova

276. Orangery Fountain:
*Triton Tearing Open the
Jaws of a Sea Monster.*
Early 18th century,
sculptor: Antonio Tarsia

277. Ramp. Entrance to
the Lower Park

278. Side Gallery

279. State Hall

280. Monplaisir Palace.
1714–1723, architects:
Johann Braunstein,
Jean-Baptiste Leblond,
Niccolo Michetti,
sculptor: Carlo
Bartolomeo Rastrelli.
Designed by Peter I.
Monplaisir Garden.
1714–1739, gardener:
Leonard Garnichfeldt.
Designed by Peter I

275

276

by the fountains make Peterhof an open-air museum unlike any other in the world.

Peter I's favourite abode was the palace of Monplaisir, which is situated close to the sea and blends harmoniously with the coastal landscape. Adjoining the central part of this one-storey building crowned with a tall roof are two glass-walled galleries, which form a delightful promenade from which both the park and the sea can be viewed. The main room of this cosy little palace is the State Hall, which appears quite large due to its eight metre high ceiling.

277

Splendid banquets and rowdy gatherings were often held here. Today, the only reminder of these "assemblies" is the enormous Great Eagle Cup, which was passed to guests who were obliged, under strict surveillance and at great risk to their health, to drain it in one go.

In the western part of the Lower Park, is the Marly ensemble the beauty and individuality of which win the hearts of all visitors to Peterhof. It was named in honour

278

279

280

281

282

281. Marly Palace and its gardens. Bird's-eye view

282. Bell Fountain. 1732, architect: Mikhail Zemtsov

283. Golden Hill Cascade. 1722–1725, architects: Niccolo Michetti, Johann Braunstein, Mikhail Zemtsov and Timofei Usov, sculptor: Carlo Bartolomeo Rastrelli, engineer: Paul Sualem

284. Marly Palace. 1720–1723, architect: Johann Braunstein

285. An avenue in the Lower Park

283

284

285

287

of its prototype, Marly le Rois, the residence of the French king, Louis XIV. The Peterhof Marly comprises three gardens (one of which is a water garden), the Golden Hill Cascade and, of course, several fountains.

The Hermitage Pavilion (a title derived from the French for an anchorite's hut) is situated in the part of the Lower Park that is closest to the sea. On the first floor is the Upper Stateroom, where evening music recitals and intimate suppers were held. Its main feature was a special table with a system of hoists. It seated 14 people and was served from the Pantry on the ground floor.

288

286. Hermitage Pavilion. 1721–1757, architects: Johann Braunstein, Bartolomeo Francesco Rastrelli

287. Upper Stateroom

288, 289. Chessboard Hill (Dragon Cascade). 1737–1739, architects: Mikhail Zemtsov, Ivan Blank, I. Davydov; sculptor: Hans Konrad Osner

289

291

292

Rastrelli played a fundamental role in transforming the Upper Chambers, built back in the Petrine era, into the impressive formal edifice known today as the Great Palace. The central three-storey component is linked by ground floor galleries to the two-storey side wings. To the west is the Coat of Arms Wing, so named because of the traditional emblem of the two-headed eagle perched atop the domed roof of the building. The coat of arms is 27 metres off the ground and a special device enables it to rotate like a weather vane. The figure of the eagle is ingeniously contrived: the presence of an extra head enables it to appear in all its double-headed glory no matter which way it turns. To the east, the architectural composition terminates in the Church, which is crowned with a central dome and a number of smaller gilded

290. Coat of Arms Wing. Detail of the cupola

291. View of the Coat of Arms Wing from the Neptune Fountain

292. Decorative sculptures in the Upper Garden

293. Peterhof. Sts Peter and Paul Cathedral. 1895–1904, architect: Nikolai Sultanov

294. Cottage Palace. Empress's Drawing Room

295. A. Maliukov. *Portrait of Empress Alexandra Fiodorovna*. 1826

296. Franz Krüger. *Portrait of Nicholas I*. 1850

297. Alexandria Park. Cottage Palace. 1826–1842, architects: Adam Menelaws, Andrei Stackenschneider

cupolas. In front of the south wall of the Great Palace stretches the Upper Park. This plot of 15 hectares, divided into equal parts, is a marvellous example of regular landscape gardening. The main garden is framed with borders and hedges and encompasses four trelliswork summerhouses and four arbours. The fountains, however, play the most important part in the decorations of the garden, the most magnificent of which is the Neptune Fountain reflecting the popular theme of the sea. The centrepiece of this three-tiered fountain is the bearded bronze figure of Neptune, the ruler of the waves. In his hands he holds a trident, the typical attribute of his power, while on his head

294

295

296

297

he wears a crown. At water level, statuesque horsemen seek to restrain plunging hippocampi surrounded by dolphins, dragons and Tritons, the escorts of the god of the sea.

At the beginning of the 19th century to the east of Petrine Peterhof an extensive landscaped park began to take shape, marked with its own distinctive architectural features. Of these, probably the most striking is the Cottage, built by Adam Menelaws for Nicholas I and his wife Alexandra Fiodorovna, in whose honour the grounds came to be known as the Alexandria Park. English Gothic motifs with a highly romantic flavour were used to decorate the building both inside and out. English rural dwellings served as the prototype on which the Cottage is based: the heir apparent had been struck by the practicality and patriarchal comfort of such houses during a visit to England. Each of the rooms of the small, cosy palace boasts its own mural, which reflects the purpose of the chamber itself. All of these works, the most notable of which is the scene decorating the Staircase, were painted by the master of monumental decorative art, Scotti. Intricate stuccowork also plays an important part in the overall design of the interiors, lending them an extraordinary elegance and charm. The house was a particular favourite of the royal family. Here, the Empress ruled the roost. Alexandra Fiodorovna's tastes were readily apparent in the décor of the rooms and the arrangement of the furniture: she personally selected the objects of applied art and paintings that were used to brighten the surroundings. Through her care and attention the Cottage became a genuine family home where the Emperor was able quite simply to be a loving husband and solicitous father. He even liked to refer to himself as the "Lord of the Cottage".

Work began on the construction of the Sts Peter and Paul Cathedral in Peterhof on 25 July 1895. The building was designed by the architect Sultanov, whose works incorporated unique embodiments of the traditions of Old Russian architecture. In his own words, "the motifs of the façade were inspired by the forms used in Russian churches of the 16th and 17th centuries, characterised by their particular richness and beauty."

298. Panorama of the Great
Palace and Grand Cascade

299. Catherine Palace.
1752–1756, architect:
Bartolomeo Francesco
Rastrelli, sculptor: Johann
Dunker

300. Cupolas of the palace
church

300

TSARSKOYE SELO

Tsarskoye Selo is associated primarily with the names of two Empresses, Elizabeth Petrovna and Catherine the Great. The initial development of the site began under Catherine I, Peter the Great's wife, who was given the land by the Emperor. However, it was only during the reign of her daughter, Elizabeth, and through the efforts of Francesco Bartolomeo Rastrelli, who believed that palaces should be created "for the common glory of Russia", that this residence could rightfully be called Tsarskoye Selo – the Tsar's Village.

301

301. Georg Kaspar
von Prenner. *Portrait
of Empress Elizabeth
Petrovna.* 1754

302. Grand Hall

303. Picture Hall

304. Main Staircase

305. Perspective view
of the suite of state rooms
(known as the Golden
Enfilade)

302

303

Besides staterooms, drawing rooms and living quarters, Rastrelli incorporated a chapel into his designs for the palace. It became known as the Church of the Resurrection and stood in the east wing of the building. The foundations of the chapel were laid with great pomp in the presence of the Royal family. Rastrelli's work as an interior designer can best be judged by the décor of the Grand Hall. This enormous room with an area of 846 square metres is permeated with a sense of greatness and majesty. Bright and airy, it seems even larger than it actually is because of the many mirrors, the abundance of gilding and, in particular, the spectacular painted ceiling, which creates an illusion of endless space. Rastrelli wanted the room to be perceived as an integral whole, so he concealed the stoves necessary to heat this huge hall behind false windows with mirrored glass.

306

One of the main features of the palace was, without a doubt, the famous Amber Room. In 1717, small amber boards and four amber panels were sent as a gift to Peter I by the Prussian king, Frederick I. Anyone who ever saw the Amber Room was enchanted by it. One French author once wrote that: "The eye, unused to seeing amber in such quantities, is captivated and blinded by the wealth and warmth of the tones, which encompass every shade of yellow, from dusky topaz to bright lemon…"

On 31 May 2003, the jubilee of St Petersburg, the ceremony of the inauguration of the Amber Room was held. The unique interior with its fine decor celebrating the beauty of the "sunny stone", has become the culminating accomplishment of the stonecutter's art of the past and present.

307

308

309

306, 309. Details
of the carved decor

307. Mask in the upper
part of the amber panel

308. Amber Room

310. Interior detail
of the room

311. Casket. 1705.
Amber, wood, metal.
By G. Turau, Germany

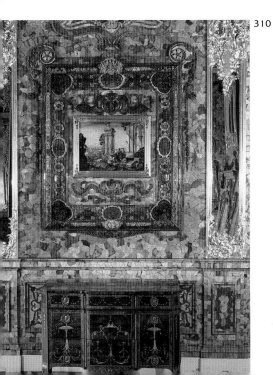

310

311

312

313

The Empress Catherine II devoted much time and care to the development of the estate and "here her genius and fine taste were revealed". "Travelling to Tsarskoye with a small retinue, Catherine divided her time between affairs of state and all manner of amusements. Every day she would take a walk in the park in the company of the knights and maids of the court... Of all the country residences, Catherine's favourite was Tsarskoye Selo. From 1763 onwards, with the exception of 2–3 years, she lived in Tsarskoye Selo in spring and spent practically all summer here, leaving in the autumn when the weather grew cold. It is here that she celebrated almost every one of her birthdays, and from here that she set out on her ceremonial journey to Petersburg on 28 June 1763 after the coronation in Moscow" (Serguei Vilchkovsky).

Under Catherine II, the vast park with an area of 100.5 hectares became a "pantheon of Russian greatness". The unique ensemble of monuments, which includes the Chesma Column and the Column of Morea, the Kagul Obelisk and the Crimean

Column, commemorates the Turkish campaigns of the 1770s and 80s, the crowning glory of the Russian forces. Around the same time, buildings that now constitute stylish monuments to Russian Classicism were also erected in the Catherine Park. The largest and most illustrious of these is the Cameron Gallery, named after its designer. The Gallery and the adjoining Agate Rooms, Cold Bath, Hanging Gardens and Ramp make up a harmonious "Greco-Roman rhapsody". Indeed, this architectural composition, which comprises several buildings created to serve a variety of functions, is inspiring for its grandeur, originality and the boldness of its design. The Cameron Gallery, intended for meditation, promenades, social intercourse and contemplation of the splendid landscape that stretches out on all sides, plays an important part in the ensemble. The architect chose a truly appropriate spot for it on the slope of the hill leading down to the Great Pond. The ground floor of the Gallery is made of massive stone blocks. Here were the living quarters for courtiers. The bright, glass-faced hall on the first floor, surrounded on all sides by a colonnade, seems still lighter and airier in comparison to the solid ground floor. The magnificent outer staircase with its elegantly curving flight of steps is a wonderful architectural creation in its own right. The two-storey building of the Agate Rooms is angled towards

312. Cameron Gallery. 1784–1787, architect: Charles Cameron

313. View of the Agate Rooms and Catherine Palace

314. Agate Rooms. Great Hall

315. View from the Cameron Gallery of the Large Pond and Grotto Pavilion. *Hercules.* 1786. Copy of an ancient original. Cast after the model of Fiodor Gordeyev

316

317

318. Catherine Park.
Palladian Bridge.
1772–1774, architect:
Vasily Neyelov

317. Alexander Park.
Chinese Village.
1782–1798, architects:
Antonio Rinaldi,
Vasily Neyelov,
Charles Cameron;
1817–1822, architect:
Vasily Stasov

318. Catherine Park.
Granite Terrace.
1809–1810, architect:
Luigi Rusca

318

the sun just as Roman thermal baths were. On the lower floor are the Cold Baths for which Cameron devised a special plumbing system. The second floor is occupied by the Agate Rooms themselves, named after the material with which the walls, columns and pilasters are covered (they are also faced with jasper). The interiors of all the rooms are amazing for the harmonious combination of architecture, painting and sculpture.

Besides the palace and the Gallery, the Catherine Park contains a number of small pavilions, which serve various purposes. One of these was the Hermitage, intended for the Empress Elizabeth amusement and solitary leisure. Often located on the shores of a pond or lake, they are magically reflected in the still surface of the waters.

319. Great Pond.
Bird's-eye view

320. Alexander Park.
Cross Bridge.
1776–1779, architect:
Vasily Neyelov

321. Catherine Park.
Hermitage Pavilion.
1749–1754, architect:
Bartolomeo Francesco
Rastrelli

321

In the 1770s, the architect Neyelov erected a remarkable bridge over the Great Pond. It was initially referred to as the Siberian Marble Gallery, since its component parts were prepared in Ekaterinburg from marble mined in the Urals and delivered to Tsarskoye Selo, where they were assembled over a period of two years. It subsequently came to be known as the Palladian Bridge in honour of the famous Italian architect and theoretician, Andrea Palladio.

The Chinoiserie style found its embodiment at Tsarskoye Selo in a number of bridges in the Catherine Park and, in particular, in the ensemble known as the Chinese Village. The latter comprises 10 houses with intricate lines and decorative curved roofs. Situated in the Alexander Park, this complex is linked to the Catherine Park by two bridges. One of these is the Great Caprice, which constitutes a unique work of park architecture. The bridge is crowned with an elegant pagoda in which the European form of the octagonal rotunda is combined with an Eastern-style upturned roof. The second is the Cross Bridge, a fascinating structure consisting of two intersecting spans. On the bridge itself stands an octagonal pavilion with a curved roof, which sports an ornamental spike topped with a sphere.

Tsarskoye Selo is not simply dear to Russians because it was one of the imperial country residences for many years. This place is also inseparably linked to the name of the great Russian poet Alexander Pushkin, who studied at the Lyceum (now a museum) and continued to visit the village at various times throughout his life. Even people who have not been to Tsarskoye Selo can clearly picture its various features and get a feel for their charms when reading the poet's verses.

In the mid-18th century, the main entrance to the palace was located on the south side of the building. A large courtyard was laid out before it, surrounded by a decorative fence with gilded details. The gateway was crowned with the Russian coat of arms. Beyond the bounds of the main estate at Tsarskoye Selo lies another famous park. The Alexander Park was laid out in the early 19th century with landscaped gardens and walkways.

322. Panorama of the Catherine Palace
and parks of Tsarskoye Selo

ИМПЕРАТОРꙊ ПАВЛꙊ Iмꙋ
ОсновательюПавловска

1872 года

PAVLOVSK

The park and palace ensemble of Pavlovsk is situated just south of Tsarskoye Selo. In 1777, Catherine II made a gift of the extensive hunting grounds along the banks of the Slavianka River to her son Paul, and two years later work began on the construction of a formal palace and the landscaping of the natural environs. Created within a relatively short space of time (from the late 1770s to the early 1800s), it became the only country estate on the outskirts of Petersburg to have complete stylistic integrity.

323. Statue of Paul I in front of Pavlovsk Palace. 1872

324. Pavlovsk Palace. 1782–1786, architect: Charles Cameron; 1786–1799, architect: Vincenzo Brenna; 1800–1825, architects: Giacomo Quarenghi, Andrei Voronikhin, Carlo Rossi

The crown prince, Paul Petrovich, and his wife, Maria Fiodorovna, put a great deal of effort into turning their family nest into one of Europe's most beautiful palaces. Within the walls of their residence they assembled an extensive collection of paintings, porcelain, ornamental metalwork and furniture. The Great Throne Room (Dining Room) situated in the south wing of the

325. Pavlovsk Palace. Egyptian Vestibule

326. Maria Fiodorovna's Library. Detal

327. Italian Hall

328. Great Throne Room. Girandole. Late 18th century. Imperial Glass Works, St Petersburg

329. Gobelin Study

330. Great Throne Room (State Dining Room)

328

palace is the work of the architect Brenna. It is here that Paul I received the knights of the Order of Malta. Today, the imperial tableware is on display in the Great Throne Room, including the famous Gold Dinner Service comprised of over 600 pieces.

329

330

331

333. Old Sylvia. Statue: *Apollo of Belvedere.* 1798. Copy of an ancient original. Cast by Edmonde Gastecloux

334. Statue: *Erminia.* Mid-19th century, sculptor: Rinaldo Rinaldi

335. Apollo Colonnade. 1782–1783, architect: Charles Cameron

336. Monument to Maria Fiodorovna. 1914, sculptor: Vladimir Beklemishev

337. Peel Tower. 1795–1797, architect: Vincenzo Brenna, designed by Pietro Gonzago

338. Temple of Friendship. 1780–1782, architect: Charles Cameron

339. Visconti Bridge. 1802–1803, architect: Andrei Voronikhin, built by C. Visconti

332

331. View of the palace and the Centaur Bridge

332. Pavilion of the Three Graces. 1800–1801, architect: Charles Cameron

The original idea and the general concept behind the layout of the main areas of the park, which now covers an area of 600 hectares, were conceived by Charles Cameron. Work began in 1782 with the laying of the main pathways leading from the palace, around which a stretch of regular park was created. Over ten pavilions were erected during the first stage of the creation of the ensemble designed by Cameron, which subsequently became the

333

334

335

336

337

338

339

compositional centrepieces of various corners of the park. The most notable of these is the Temple of Friendship, the architect's first work in Russia. He built the rotunda on a small peninsula and encircled it with a ring of 16 columns. The Temple of Friendship, which presents a gorgeous sight from a variety of viewpoints, is a wonderful complement to the romantic beauty of the landscape. Cameron's last architectural contribution to Pavlovsk was the Pavilion of the Three Graces, a portico in the guise of an ancient temple. Its pediments are decorated with high reliefs depicting the gods Apollo and Minerva (sculptor: Ivan Prokofiev). The edifice was given its current title in 1803 when a sculptural group by Paolo Triscorni showing three female figures supporting a vase was installed inside. Cameron envisaged Pavlovsk Park as the abode of the god and patron of the arts, Apollo, and the refuge of the Muses. The architect erected the so-called Apollo Colonnade almost at the entrance to the park from the Tsarskoye Selo side, a horse-shoe-shaped structure somewhat akin to a Classical rotunda with a double row of sturdy columns crowned by the vault of the heavens. The material chosen for this work was grey limestone, the coarseness of which was intended to give the impression that the monument dated from a bygone era. In the centre of the colonnade stands a statue of Apollo Belvedere (1782, cast from a mould of the antique original).

A large part in the design of the park was played by Pietro di Gottardo Gonzago, who also contributed to the palace interiors. He created entire landscaped areas that highlighted the inherent beauty of the natural surroundings themselves. As an architect and set designer, Gonzago devised a special system for planting trees and shrubs based on the different times at which they bloomed and faded to ensure that the park would be a riot of colour from early spring to late autumn, in other words the entire time that the members of the royal family would be inhabiting the summer residence.

Pavlovsk Park is characterised by the highly original and diverse artistic trends in park and garden design that prevail within its confines.

340. Panorama of Pavlovsk Palace

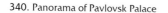

KONSTANTINOVSKY PALACE

The fate of the palace and grounds at Strelna is a remarkable phenomenon in the annals of St Petersburg's history. The high status intended for the residence was reflected in the amount of planning and construction that went into it in the first quarter of the 18th century, and its importance can really only be fully appreciated when we recall Peter's grandiose scheme for an ideal town on the shores of the Gulf of Finland. Fate was capricious with this pet project of the tsar, as is seen in the decline of the residence in the course of the 18th century, its retreat into the shadow of grand-ducal status for one and a half centuries, teetering on imperial status in the 19th, only to be swept away altogether by the revolution in the 20th. In the year St Petersburg celebrated its tercentenary, the Konstaninovsky Palace at Strelna was reborn.

A semicircular arrival zone in front of the palace, like the main palace terrace, has granite paving laid out in a traditional Italian pattern and is lined with the flags of countries represented at international meetings. In the centre there is an equestrian statue of Peter the Great, a replica

341, 345. Konstantinovsky Palace. 1720–1730, architect: Niccolo Michetti

342. Panoramic view of the villa township

343. Equestrian statue of Peter the Great. Copy of Gustav Schmidt Kassel's statue unveiled in Riga in 1910 to commemorate Russia's annexation of Livonia. Bronze, granite

344. Russia–EC Summit. Heads of state in the Blue Hall. 31 May 2003

344

345

346

of German sculptor Gustav Schmidt Kassel's 1910 statue commissioned to mark the bicentenary of Russia's annexation of Livonia.

The decor in Grand Duke Konstantin Konstantinovich's Study is based on written accounts and photographs from the 1910s. The Meander Drawing Room took its name from the main decorative feature of the room, the meander pattern (also known as the Greek key pattern), which is painted here in so-called "grisaille" style, a monochrome technique imitating bas-relief.

346. Marble Hall

347. Blue Hall

348. Music Room

349. Belvedere Hall

347

34

349

350

The Blue Hall has been the venue for a range of events from meetings and conferences to formal dinners and fashion parades. The Marble Hall is in the very centre of the palace. When not in use, the conference table is left set up as it was for the heads of delegations to the "Russia–EC" summit, in memory of this historic event at the Konstantinovsky Palace. The Music Room and Pink Dining Room share a common architectural history and have complementary decor. The Belvedere Hall is 31 metres above the level of the Baltic Sea. This modern interior replaces the former attic, which in the 19th century had steps leading up to the belvedere tower. This was Grand Duke Konstantin Pavlovich's favourite place, ideal for inspecting the manoeuvres of the guards, for which a sofa and small table with telescope were at hand. The Belvedere Hall is furnished in the style of salon-cabins on Russian imperial yachts, adapted to the particular shape of this interior. The north wall is entirely taken up by a panoramic window looking out towards St Petersburg, Kronstadt and the Baltic horizon. Poised over the main armchairs in the hall, as if to inspire participants in meetings here, there is a carved and gilded galley-prow depicting Nike with victor's wreath, otherwise known as "Winged Victory".

350. Grand Duke Konstantin
Konstantinovich's Study

351. Meander Drawing Room

352. Pink Dining Room

351

352

Contents

Preface	5
Peter and Paul Fortress	11
Sts Peter and Paul Cathedral	15
Vasilievsky Island	24
Stock Exchange. *Kunstkammer*	28
Menshikov Palace	30
Academy of Arts	31
Vasilievsky Island – the maritime heart of St Petersburg	32
Admiralty	34
Decembrists Square	36
St Isaac's Square. St Isaac's Cathedral	38
Mariinsky Palace	49
Palace Square. State Hermitage Museum	51
Nevsky Prospekt	68
Kazan Cathedral	70
Pushkin's Apartment	72
Russian Museum	74
Ostrovsky Square and Yeliseev's shop	80
Anichkov Bridge	82
Beloselsky-Belozersky Palace	83
Field of Mars	84
Church on the Spilled Blood (Church of the Resurrection)	86
Mikhailovsky Castle	92
Summer Gardens	94
Marble Palace	96
Yusupov Palace	97
Mariinsky Theatre	98
St Nicholas Cathedral	100
St Alexander Nevsky Monastery	102
Holy Trinity Cathedral	103
St Petersburg Churches	105
Smolny Monastery	107
Great October Revolution	109
Siege of Leningrad	110
Bridges of St Petersburg	112
White Nights	114
Peterhof	119
Tsarskoye Selo	135
Pavlovsk	147
Konstantinovsky Palace	154

SAINT PETERSBURG

Ivan Fiodorov Art Publishers
11 Zvenigorodskaya St, St Petersburg, 191119 Russia
Tel./fax: +7 (812) 320 9201, 320 9211
E-mail: info@p-2.ru
Ivan Fiodorov Printing Company (6741)
PRINTED AND BOUND IN RUSSIA

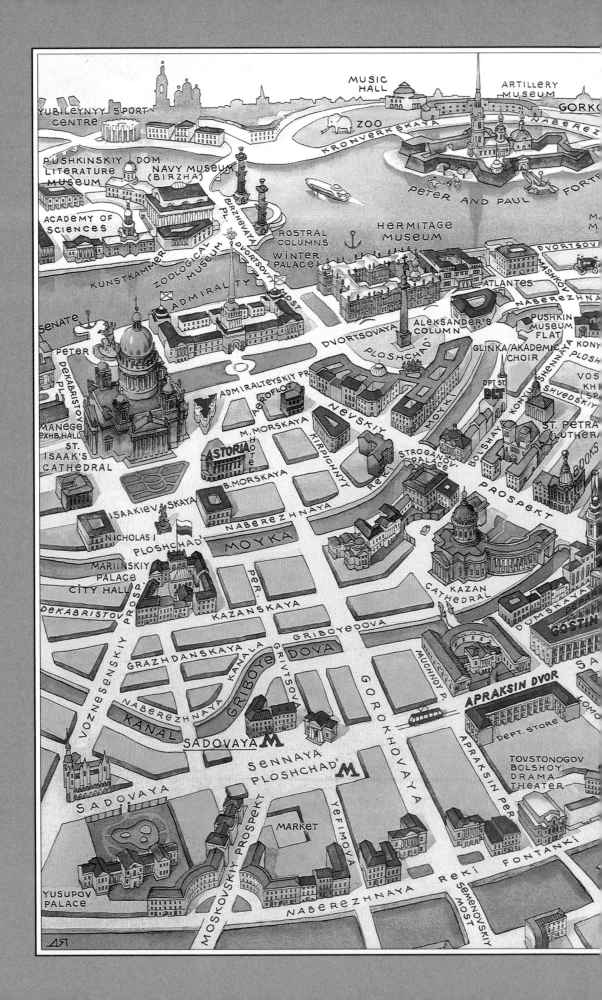